DEPARTMENT OF TRANSPORT

Transport Statistics Report

ROAD ACCIDENT STATISTICS ENGLISH REGIONS 1994

Published July 1995

London: HMSO

Prepared for publication by STD5 branch
Directorate of Statistics
Department of Transport

Richard Ackroyd
Paul O'Connor
Linden Francis
Paula Budge

GOVERNMENT STATISTICAL SERVICE

A service of statistical information and advice is provided to the government by specialist staff employed in the statistics divisions of individual Departments. Statistics are made generally available through their publications and further information and advice on them can be obtained from the Departments concerned.

Enquiries about the contents of this publication should be made to:

Directorate of Statistics
Department of Transport
Room B648
Romney House
43 Marsham Street
London SW1P 3PY

Telephone 0171 276 8785 - Fax 0171 276 8269

Data Service

Copies of the main tables in this publication can be supplied on a computer diskette by the Department of Transport (at a cost of £40). Further tabulations of road accident statistics are also available from the Department, subject to confidentiality rules. The charges vary with the complexity of the analysis (minimum £40) and the availability of these services depends upon the resources within the Department. Enquiries should be addressed in writing to Mr P S O'Connor at the above address

Contents

Symbols and Conventions

Rounding of Figures:

In tables where figures have been rounded there may be an apparent slight discrepancy between the sum of the constituent items and the independently rounded total.

Symbols:

'..' = not available

Conversion Factor:

1 kilometre = 0.6214 mile

Preface

This edition of Road Accident Statistics English Regions (RASER) gives statistics of road accidents on a local basis for England in the years up to 1994. RASER concentrates on accidents as being incidents which may reflect a need for local action and is intended to be of most benefit to traffic engineers, planners and administrators in local government and the Government Offices for the Regions. For this reason, most of the data in the book are compiled according to the county groupings covered by these offices. Please see the commentary on the tables and charts for information on the restructuring of the Regional Office organisation.

RASER includes only background national statistics, so it should be regarded as a supplement to 'Road Accidents Great Britain 1994 - The Casualty Report' (RAGB), which is the main publication on road accident statistics in Great Britain. RAGB 1994 is available from HMSO bookshops, price £12.00.

The current system of collecting road accident statistics was set up in 1968, and is for the benefit and use of local authorities, the police and central government. Each year, about 230,000 STATS19 road accident report forms (an example of which can be found on pages 41 to 43) are completed by police officers of the 51 police forces in Great Britain. These forms record data about accidents on the public highway which involved personal injury or death. These data are transferred onto magnetic tape or computer diskette and are sent to DOT where they are incorporated into an annual data file.

The principal purpose in collecting and publishing statistics of road accidents is to provide background information for both central government and local authorities on the roads, road users, places, times of day, weather conditions, where road accidents happen etc, and against which various remedial measures can be considered. Road accident statistics are used to provide both a local and a national perspective for particular road safety problems or particular suggested remedies. A continuous flow of information - such as the time series tables in this book - means that trends of accidents and casualties can be examined and used to change the direction of policies when necessary.

The report also includes data from Northern Ireland. These data, where available, are included with each table along with data for Scotland and Wales. *More detailed statistics for Scotland and Wales are available from the Scottish and Welsh Offices - please refer to the inside rear cover for more details.*

Several of the tables contain averages of 1981-85 data. These represent the base figures which the Secretary of State for Transport used to set the target of reducing the number of road casualties by one third by the year 2000. It should also be noted that main Tables 1 and 6 which give casualty totals by severity for the years covering 1981 to 1985 have been extended to show revised estimates for London for this period. At the beginning of September 1984 the Metropolitan police implemented improved procedures for allocating the level of severity to accidents and casualties. The change is thought to have had no effect on overall casualty numbers, but in the period between 1981 and the date of the change it is estimated that there were 4,725 casualties whose injuries were originally judged to be slight but would have been judged serious under the later procedures. However, this is an overall estimate and it is not possible to present similar revised estimates of accidents by road type and other detailed characteristics.

DOT is generally prepared to sell tabulations of road accident data. The cost of data varies with the complexity of each request, but averages about £40 per year of data. Further information can be obtained from: - *Mr Paul O'Connor, Department of Transport, Room B648, Romney House, 43 Marsham Street, London SW1P 3PY, Telephone 0171-276-8785.*

1. Commentary on tables and charts

Richard Ackroyd

Introduction

This section gives a review of the tables and charts included in this report. As noted in the preface, and with the exception of table 15, the data are disaggregated either by county or Department of Transport (DOT) region, and Northern Ireland data have been included within certain tables. Tables where Northern Ireland data are not available, and thus where no United Kingdom total can be given, have been individually annotated.

From April 1994, the DOT regional offices were subsumed within the Government Offices for the Regions. However, as this was a mid-year change and in order to keep the figures on a consistent basis with those in previous editions of RASER, the main body of tables give figures on the basis of the previous regional structure. The constituent counties of the former DOT regions can be found in table 14 on pages 31 to 35. The changes to the regional organisation, as they affect this report, will be reviewed later this year and, if necessary, implemented in RASER 1995.

As reported in *Road Accident Statistics English Regions 1992*, from April 1991 responsibility for the county of Cumbria transferred from the North West region of the DOT organisation to the Northern region. The DOT accident database was amended with effect from January 1992 and as a consequence the numbers and rates for 1992 to 1994 as shown in this report have been based on the amended organisation, but for the years up to and including 1991 the old definition has been used.

In order to provide consistent time series, the casualty data for the Northern and North West regions in **table 1** have been calculated throughout according to the above regional definition. The data for previous years in these two regions in **table 14** have also been similarly revised. However, the change in definition means that in the remaining tables the data for 1992-1994 for these regions are not consistent with data for previous years.

It should also be noted that population figures as used throughout this report are final mid-1993 estimates. Mid-year estimates for 1994 were not available at the time of going to publication.

Casualties

Table 1 gives the regional distribution of casualties and is presented as a time series for the period 1987 to 1994. The average for the years 1981-1985 is also given. There has been little significant change in the aggregate casualty distribution between the regions over this period. In each of the eight years shown, London had the highest number of casualties. In the years 1987 to 1990 the next highest number of casualties was in the South East region but since 1991 the next highest number was in the North West region. The lowest number of casualties was in the Northern region, which had, under the old regional definition, and until 1991, about half those in the East Midland region, the next lowest in England. Under the revised regional definition, this proportion has fallen to a little over one third.

The table also shows that in 1994 the North West region had the highest overall casualty rate per 100,000 population, followed by London and the Eastern region. The lowest rates were found in the Northern and South West regions. London, however, had the lowest fatality rate of all the regions - probably because accidents in urban areas tend to be less severe because they occur at lower speeds. The highest fatality rate was in the East Midlands region with the next highest in the Eastern and West Midlands regions.

Chart 1a depicts the number of casualties killed and the number seriously injured in each region in 1994. The chart shows that the Eastern and South East regions had the highest number of those killed and London and the South East region the highest number of those seriously injured.

Chart 1b depicts the number of casualties killed or seriously injured (KSI) and slightly injured in each region in 1994 and shows that London had the highest number of casualties in both severity groups and the Northern region and Wales the lowest number.

Chart 2 depicts the number of child casualties per 100,000 child population in each region in 1994 and shows that Scotland had the highest rate of children killed or seriously injured and the South East and South West regions the lowest rate. The North West region had the highest overall rate of child casualties.

Chart 3 shows the number of adult casualties per 100,000 population in each region in 1994 and shows that Scotland had the highest rate of adults killed or seriously injured and the Northern region the lowest rate. The London and the North West region had the highest overall rate of adult casualties.

Charts 4 and **5** depict the percentage change in overall casualties and those killed or seriously injured for each region between 1993 and 1994 (the charts take account of the change in regional definition as noted in the introduction). **Chart 4** shows that overall casualties have risen in all but one, London, of the nine English regions and in Scotland and Wales. The **Chart 5** shows that casualties killed or seriously injured fell in five English regions, with the largest fall, at 8 per cent, recorded in the South West region.

Local authority casualty comparisons

Tables 2-5 give information on the number of casualties, rate per 100,000 population, and percentage distribution, by age and road user type for each English county, Scotland and Wales.

Table 2 gives the number of casualties by age and road user type for 1994 and **Table 3** gives the same information as an average for the years 1981-1985.

Table 4 gives casualty rates, per 100,000 population, by age and by type of road user for each English county. In England in 1994, 390 children were killed or injured in road accidents per 100,000 children and the county casualty rates varied from 253 in Avon to 545 in Merseyside. The casualty rate for those aged 60 and over varied from 172 in Avon to 364 in Cambridgeshire. The overall casualty rate for all ages was lowest in Avon and highest in Surrey. The pedestrian casualty rate was highest in most urbanised areas, in particular London, Greater Manchester and Merseyside, and lowest in rural counties such as Oxfordshire and Suffolk. The pedal cyclist casualty rate was highest in Cambridgeshire and lowest in Durham and Tyne & Wear. The car occupant casualty rate varied from 216 in Avon and Tyne & Wear to 510 in Surrey.

Table 5 gives the distribution of casualties, by age and by type of road user, for each county. In England in 1994, 14 per cent of road accident casualties were children and 10 per cent were aged 60 and over. The proportion of casualties who were children varied from 11 per cent in Cambridgeshire, Dorset, Gloucestershire, Surrey and Wiltshire to 20 per cent in Cleveland. East Sussex had the highest proportion of casualties aged 60 or over; 16 per cent compared with 10 per cent in the whole of England.

Table 6 gives the number of casualties killed or seriously injured and total casualties in each English county for 1994 and compares them with the average for the years 1981-1985. The percentage change is also given. In England as a whole, the number killed or seriously has fallen by 37 per cent and overall casualties by 1 per cent. The number of casualties killed or seriously injured has fallen in every county except Lancashire, with the largest fall, at 66 per cent, recorded in Avon.

Casualties by road type

Charts 6a and **6b** depict the number of casualties killed or seriously injured and slightly injured in each region on built-up and non built-up roads respectively. On built-up roads, the highest number of casualties for both severity groups was in London, with Wales and the Northern region having the lowest number for both severity groups. On non built-up roads, the highest number of casualties killed or seriously injured was in the Eastern region and the highest number of slight casualties was in the South East and Eastern regions. The lowest number of casualties for both severity groups was in London.

Table 7 gives the total number of casualties in each region disaggregated by severity and by road type. In each regions, over 50 per cent of casualties were in accidents on built-up roads and, except in the South East region with 6 per cent, no more than 5 per cent of casualties were in accidents on motorways. The proportion of casualties who were killed or seriously injured was highest on non-built up roads.

Charts 7 and **8** show, for built-up and non built-up roads respectively, overall casualty numbers on trunk, principal and 'other' roads in each region in 1994. On built-up roads, the highest number of casualties on trunk and principal roads was in London and the highest number of casualties on 'other' roads was in the North West region. On non built-up roads, the highest number of casualties on trunk roads and 'other' roads was in the Eastern region and the highest number of casualties on principal roads in the South East region.

Table 8 gives the casualty rates by severity for motorways and A roads for each region. The casualty rate is derived by dividing the number of casualties on a particular road type by the traffic carried on those roads. The rates are given as an average for the period 1992 to 1994. The data show that the highest 'all severities' rate on motorways was in London, with the lowest in the South West region. London also had the highest 'all severities' rate for all A roads, and the South West the lowest rate. For England as a whole, the highest 'all severities' rate was on built-up trunk and principal roads, and the lowest on motorways.

4

Accidents

Table 9 gives accident rates by severity for motorways and A roads for each region. The accident rate is derived by dividing the number of accidents on particular road types by the traffic carried on that road type. The rates are given as an average for the period 1992 to 1994. The data show that over the three year period, in England as a whole, built-up principal A roads had the highest overall accident rate at 101 accidents per 100 million vehicle kilometres and motorways the lowest rate at 11 accidents per 100 million vehicle kilometres. For fatal accidents, the respective rates for these two road types were 1.1 accidents and 0.2 accidents. The table also shows that overall and fatal or serious accident rates were higher on principal A roads than on trunk A roads.

Chart 9 depicts the number of accidents on motorways and trunk and principal A roads in each region in 1994. The chart shows that the South East region had the highest number of accidents on motorways, and London the highest number of accidents on trunk and principal A roads.

Seasonal pattern of accidents

The seasonal pattern of injury accidents is given in **Table 10**. The base has been calculated as the average number of accidents per day in each region. The peak months for accidents can vary from year to year for various reasons, for example, differing weather conditions. The general pattern is low accident numbers in the early part of the year, gradually building up to a peak in May, June and July, followed by a small dip and then a higher peak from October to December. This trend continued in 1994, when the peak month for all accidents was either October or December in all English regions except in the Northern region where the peak month was November. February or April had the lowest number of accidents in all English regions.

When accident figures are related to the number of days in each month, the lowest daily rate of all accidents was in either March or April in six of the nine English regions. The highest daily rate was again in either October or December in all English regions except in the Northern region. The pattern was similar for fatal and serious accidents, with the peak month for these accidents, both in number and by day, being either October or December in all regions except the Northern region.

Accidents by road type

Tables 11-13 show the number of junction and non-junction injury accidents occurring on motorways and trunk and principal A roads. On all motorways in England, 17 per cent of accidents occurred at junctions and roundabouts. On all trunk A roads in England, 60 per cent of accidents occurred at junctions and roundabouts as did 69 per cent of accidents on principal A roads.

Junction accidents, including those on roundabouts, accounted for about 50 per cent of all trunk A road accidents in each region except the West Midlands and East Midlands regions where the proportion was higher at about 60 per cent, and the North West and London regions, where the proportion rose to 70 cent. This pattern was repeated on principal A roads, where about 65 per cent of accidents occurred at junctions in all regions except in the North

West region where the proportion rose to 74 per cent and in London, where the proportion was 77 per cent.

Table 14 gives the total number of injury accidents disaggregated by severity on different types of road in each region and county for 1993 and 1994. The average for the years 1981 to 1985 is also given. The road classifications used are motorways, trunk and principal A roads and all roads.

Table 15 shows injury accidents and casualties by severity, and the vehicles involved, for individual English motorways, including A(M) roads. Eighty three per cent of the vehicles involved were cars or vans while 14 per cent were heavy lorries, broadly in line with their share of motorway traffic. Motorways with the highest numbers of accidents per kilometre in 1994 were the M25 (5.0 accidents) and the M63 and M23 (4.6 accidents).

Table 16 gives the percentage of accidents on the various types of road within each region. This table should be considered in conjunction with Table 19 which shows the distribution of motor traffic within each region.

Background data

Table 17 gives regional background information on road lengths, home population, area, and licensed vehicle numbers. **Table 18** gives the 1992-1994 average distribution between regions of motor traffic on major roads, and **Table 19** shows the distribution of motor traffic within each region. All road lengths shown in Tables 15 and 17 are taken from the Transport Statistics Report *'Road Lengths in Great Britain 1994'*.

List of charts and tables

CHARTS

Chart 1a: Fatal and serious casualties: by region: 1994

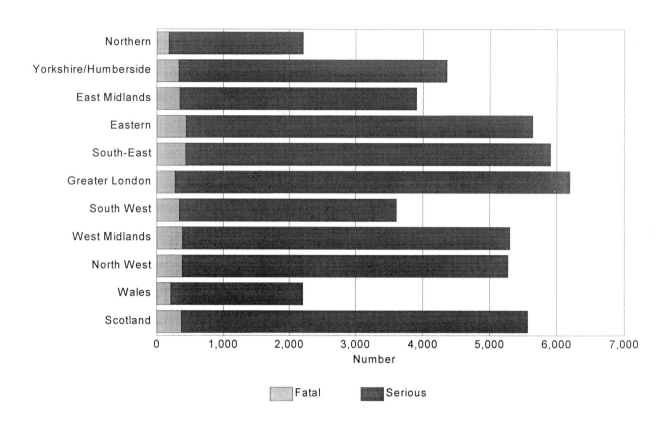

Chart 1b: KSI and slight casualties: by region: 1994

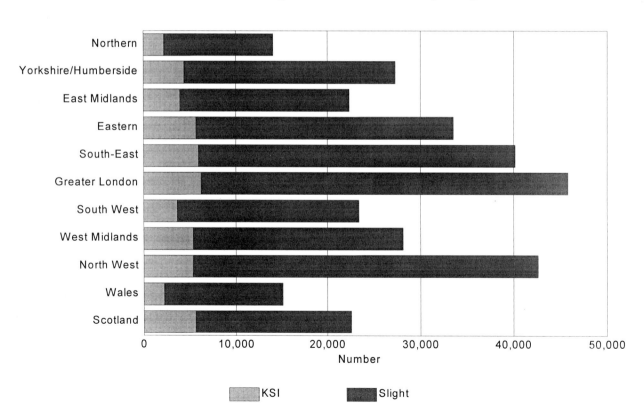

Chart 2: Child casualties per 100,000 population: by severity and region: 1994

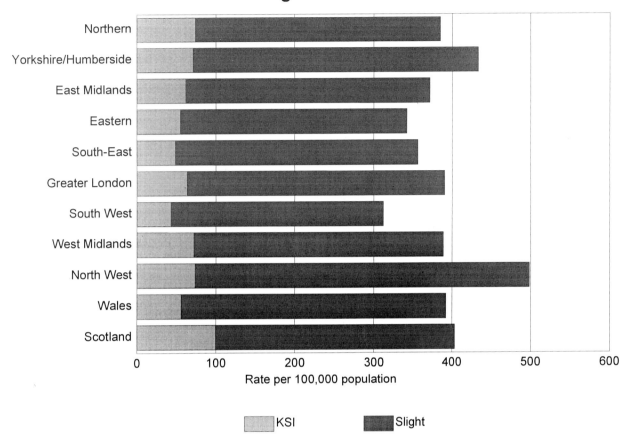

Rate per 100,000 population

KSI   Slight

Chart 3: Adult casualties per 100,000 population: by severity and region: 1994

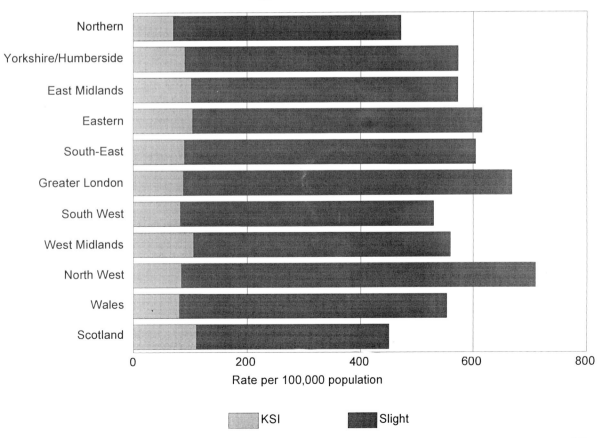

Rate per 100,000 population

KSI   Slight

11

Chart 4: Percentage change in total casualties: by region: 1993-1994

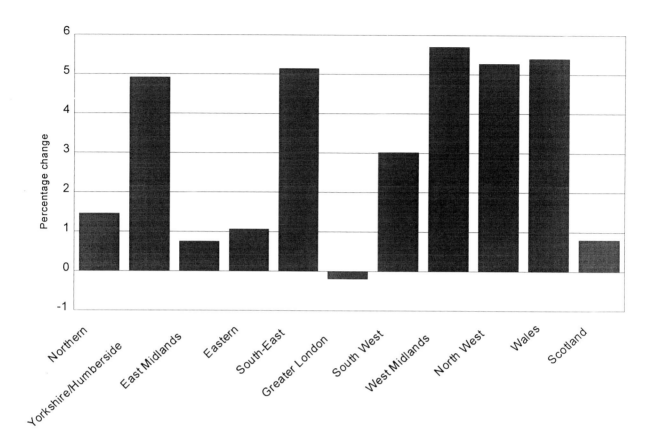

Chart 5: Percentage change in KSI casualties: by region: 1993-1994

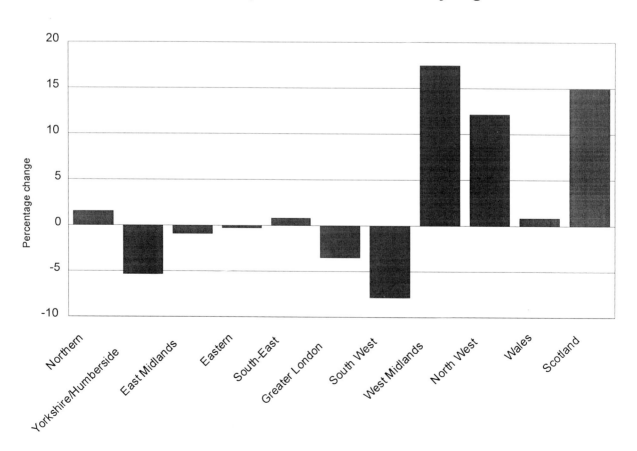

Chart 6a: Casualties on built-up roads: by severity and region: 1994

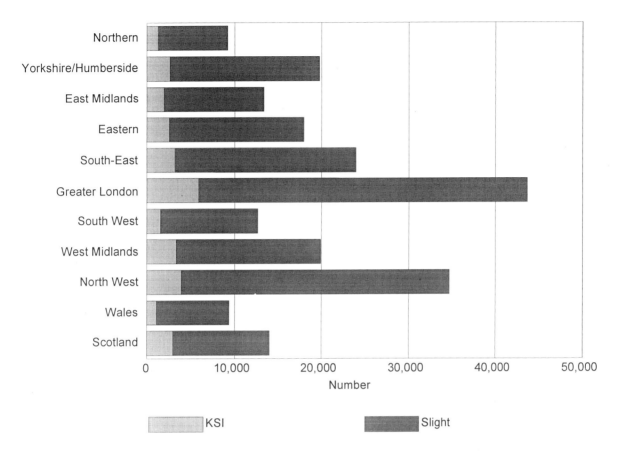

Chart 6b: Casualties on non built-up roads: by severity and region: 1994

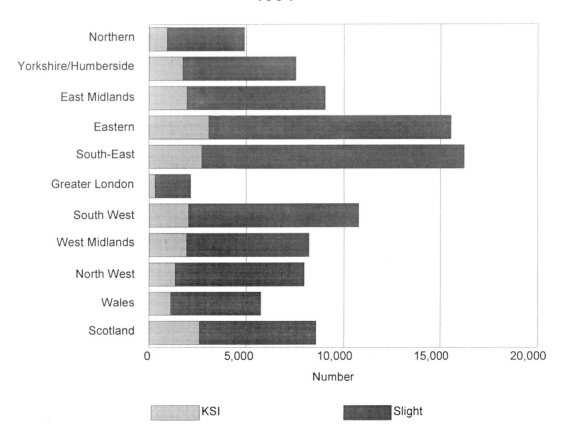

Chart 7: Casualties by road class and region: built-up roads: 1994

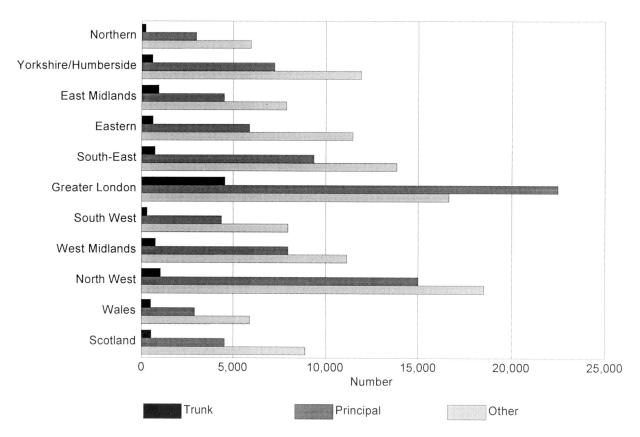

Chart 8: Casualties by road class and region: non built-up roads: 1994

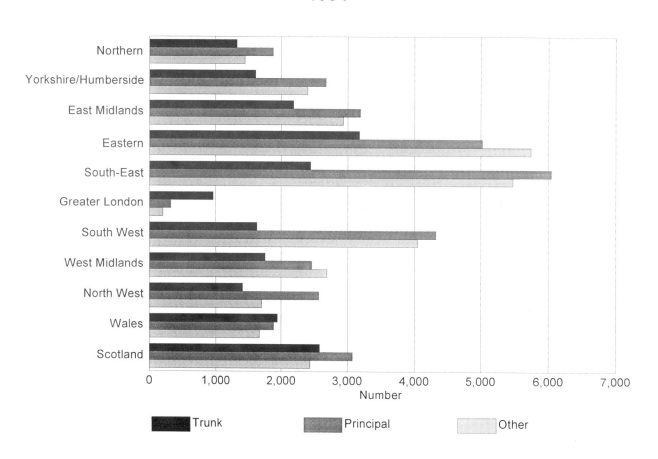

Chart 9: Accidents by road class and region: 1994

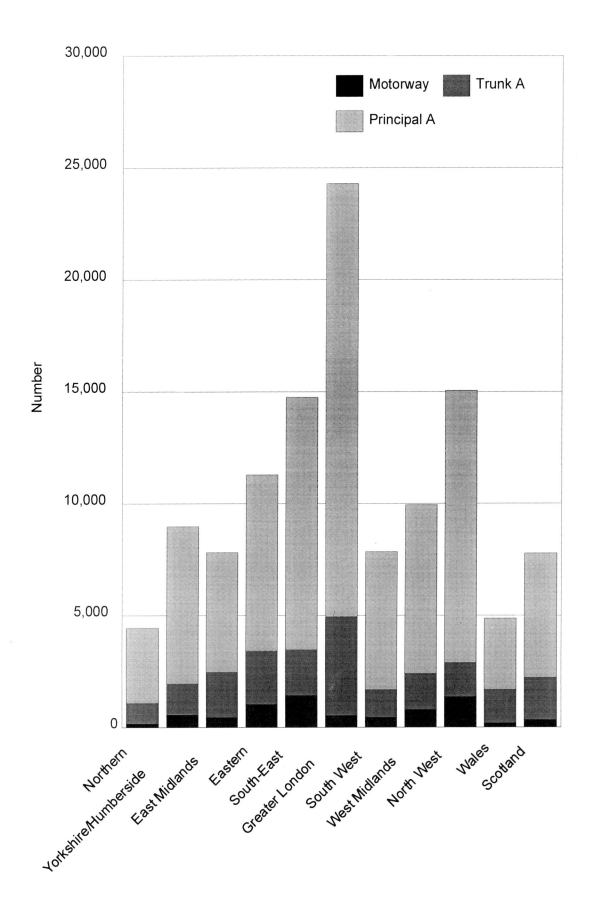

TABLES

1 Casualties: by region and severity: 1981-85 average, 1987-1994: rate per 100,000 population, 1994

Number/rate

	1981-85 Average	1987	1988	1989	1990	1991	1992	1993	1994	1994 Rate Per 100,000 Population[1]
Northern[2]										
Killed	282	294	280	270	334	287	225	230	178	5.7
Killed or seriously injured	3,566	2,916	2,947	2,962	3,050	2,651	2,475	2,178	2,212	71.3
All Casualties	13,913	13,858	14,029	15,597	16,021	14,848	14,468	13,880	14,082	453.9
Yorkshire and Humberside										
Killed	501	440	437	480	428	413	414	387	325	6.5
Killed or seriously injured	6,830	5,817	6,131	6,127	5,978	5,202	5,110	4,603	4,357	86.9
All Casualties	25,915	25,328	26,884	28,560	28,455	26,086	26,599	26,031	27,310	544.7
East Midlands										
Killed	492	448	413	514	513	410	393	350	341	8.4
Killed or seriously injured	6,389	5,254	5,031	5,342	5,045	4,173	4,145	3,940	3,905	95.6
All Casualties	23,079	22,494	23,308	25,129	24,852	22,397	22,175	22,207	22,375	548.0
Eastern										
Killed	601	614	587	617	608	546	488	455	438	7.5
Killed or seriously injured	9,312	8,318	8,230	7,967	7,653	6,287	6,132	5,656	5,640	96.5
All Casualties	33,789	35,886	37,896	39,424	37,908	33,768	33,388	33,180	33,534	573.7
South East										
Killed	735	676	718	715	699	516	496	478	427	6.0
Killed or seriously injured	11,038	9,446	9,321	8,766	8,155	6,388	6,325	5,859	5,907	83.4
All Casualties	41,999	40,326	41,184	43,050	42,387	38,211	38,876	38,225	40,191	567.2
Greater London[3]										
Killed	539	456	446	460	408	368	316	286	270	3.9
Killed or seriously injured	8,230 (9,175)	9,517	9,478	9,344	8,910	7,878	7,233	6,419	6,195	89.4
All Casualties	54,156	49,454	50,114	52,779	51,871	46,578	46,417	45,927	45,837	661.1
South West										
Killed	484	457	462	521	468	460	385	310	336	7.0
Killed or seriously injured	8,047	6,250	6,134	5,781	5,424	4,555	4,153	3,916	3,608	75.7
All Casualties	26,352	24,507	25,444	25,246	25,034	22,515	22,302	22,728	23,413	491.0
West Midlands										
Killed	526	442	442	498	478	386	395	353	382	7.2
Killed or seriously injured	7,857	5,860	5,774	6,190	6,136	5,298	4,913	4,514	5,303	100.3
All Casualties	27,699	25,425	26,760	28,964	30,219	27,425	27,089	26,599	28,114	531.5
North West[2]										
Killed	538	522	498	512	487	468	437	379	380	5.9
Killed or seriously injured	6,219	5,391	5,172	5,334	5,470	4,972	4,811	4,705	5,276	82.3
All Casualties	33,478	35,183	36,375	39,203	40,729	39,014	40,445	40,510	42,645	665.0
England										
Killed	4,698	4,349	4,283	4,587	4,423	3,854	3,549	3,228	3,077	6.3
Killed or seriously injured	67,388	58,769	58,218	57,813	55,821	47,404	45,297	41,790	42,403	87.4
All Casualties	280,382	272,461	281,994	297,952	297,476	270,842	271,759	269,287	277,501	571.8
Wales										
Killed	259	220	226	233	249	227	220	187	210	7.2
Killed or seriously injured	3,855	3,388	3,127	3,191	3,037	2,638	2,537	2,189	2,208	76.0
All Casualties	14,395	14,266	15,164	16,165	16,432	15,074	14,732	14,331	15,105	519.7
Scotland										
Killed	641	556	543	553	545	487	460	399	363	7.1
Killed or seriously injured	8,887	7,261	7,198	7,527	6,800	6,131	5,640	4,844	5,570	108.8
All Casualties	27,134	24,746	25,147	27,475	27,233	25,353	24,182	22,402	22,583	441.1
Great Britain										
Killed	5,598	5,125	5,052	5,373	5,217	4,568	4,229	3,814	3,650	6.5
Killed or seriously injured	80,130	69,418	68,543	68,531	65,658	56,173	53,474	48,823	50,181	88.7
All Casualties	321,912	311,473	322,305	341,592	341,141	311,269	310,673	306,020	315,189	557.3
Northern Ireland										
Killed	196	214	178	181	185	185	150	143	157	9.6
Killed or seriously injured	2,362	2,099	2,147	2,195	2,178	1,833	1,991	1,725	1,805	110.6
All Casualties	8,204	9,936	10,967	11,611	11,761	10,314	11,264	11,100	12,094	741.1
United Kingdom										
Killed	5,793	5,339	5,230	5,554	5,402	4,753	4,379	3,957	3,807	6.5
Killed or seriously injured	82,492	71,517	70,690	70,726	67,836	58,006	55,465	50,548	51,986	89.3
All Casualties	330,115	321,409	333,272	353,203	352,902	321,583	321,937	317,120	327,283	562.4

1 Based on final 1993 population estimates.
2 From 1st April 1991 responsibilty for Cumbria transferred from the North West Regional Office to the Northern Regional Office. The change to the road accident database was deferred until 1992. Data prior to 1992 for both Northern and North West regions have been revised to take account of the change in boundaries (see introduction on page 3).
3. In September 1984 the Metropolitan Police implemented revised standards in the assessment of serious casualties. The figure in brackets is an estimate of casualty totals under standards prevailing since 1984. See notes.

2 Number of casualties: by county, by type of road user: 1994

	Children (0-15)	Adults (16-59)	Elderly (60+)	All[1] casualties	Pedest- rians	Pedal cyclists	Motor cyclists	Car occupants	Number of casualties Other[2] road users
Avon	478	2,661	355	3,561	535	314	363	2,103	246
Bedfordshire	397	2,175	234	2,806	356	209	204	1,850	187
Berkshire	489	2,948	310	3,911	444	343	346	2,608	170
Buckinghamshire	461	2,853	334	3,785	341	251	297	2,692	204
Cambridgeshire	466	3,361	462	4,368	315	697	413	2,716	227
Cheshire	771	4,980	598	6,349	622	417	426	4,382	502
Cleveland	532	1,846	277	2,655	582	226	96	1,597	154
Cornwall	358	2,037	379	2,781	308	150	310	1,807	206
Cumbria	338	1,938	314	2,591	330	170	239	1,681	171
Derbyshire	656	3,715	498	5,097	691	328	464	3,386	228
Devon	651	3,772	616	5,040	740	372	592	3,123	213
Dorset	397	2,616	505	3,518	352	306	333	2,322	205
Durham	425	1,911	267	2,604	455	116	125	1,666	242
East Sussex	550	2,972	665	4,187	678	331	345	2,499	334
Essex	1,144	7,030	967	9,505	1,030	723	696	6,511	545
Gloucestershire	313	2,115	344	2,772	272	240	266	1,851	143
Greater London	5,430	32,943	4,080	45,837	9,594	4,408	5,495	22,618	3,722
Greater Manchester	2,906	12,483	1,483	16,872	3,188	1,177	625	10,656	1,226
Hampshire	1,158	6,815	886	8,859	971	1,035	854	5,527	472
Hereford & Worcester	453	2,701	407	3,562	413	282	302	2,286	279
Hertfordshire	667	4,584	522	5,830	526	407	450	4,167	280
Humberside	818	3,579	465	4,863	778	691	485	2,510	399
Isle of Wight	94	444	95	633	92	73	85	345	38
Kent	1,149	6,083	855	8,192	993	689	861	5,233	416
Lancashire	1,464	6,751	1,015	9,273	1,441	616	501	5,981	734
Leicestershire	672	3,571	455	4,755	672	430	362	2,974	317
Lincolnshire	462	2,647	416	3,525	307	301	322	2,318	277
Merseyside	1,675	7,433	1,043	10,151	1,691	572	347	6,767	774
Norfolk	572	3,114	528	4,389	405	361	402	2,973	248
Northamptonshire	415	2,322	317	3,056	353	198	221	2,127	157
Northumberland	245	1,057	182	1,484	170	91	84	1,004	135
North Yorkshire	594	3,585	541	4,734	425	353	402	3,211	343
Nottinghamshire	900	4,104	558	5,942	884	508	474	3,574	502
Oxfordshire	369	2,339	287	3,118	252	343	272	2,040	211
Shropshire	264	1,671	238	2,173	216	137	179	1,500	141
Somerset	295	1,725	307	2,398	225	186	191	1,690	106
South Yorkshire	1,172	4,392	620	6,185	1,154	414	359	3,696	562
Staffordshire	988	5,081	618	6,957	817	438	500	4,642	560
Suffolk	396	2,106	346	2,851	292	296	316	1,779	168
Surrey	755	5,626	729	7,567	632	626	685	5,292	332
Tyne & Wear	921	3,323	504	4,748	1,120	331	149	2,788	360
Warwickshire	371	2,460	301	3,282	326	248	243	2,242	223
West Midlands	2,253	8,706	1,181	12,140	2,775	936	648	7,060	721
West Sussex	461	2,786	477	3,724	337	391	322	2,467	207
West Yorkshire	1,903	8,449	1,176	11,528	2,340	637	561	7,195	795
Wiltshire	378	2,583	375	3,343	281	266	307	2,255	234
England	38,626	204,393	28,132	277,501	41,721	22,634	22,519	171,711	18,916
Wales	2,359	11,017	1,728	15,105	2,200	795	860	10,114	1,136
Scotland	4,166	15,907	2,508	22,583	4,732	1,384	930	13,284	2,253
Great Britain	45,151	231,317	32,368	315,189	48,653	24,813	24,309	195,109	22,305
Northern Ireland	1,749	9,341	1,004	12,094	1,271	312	247	8,893	1,371
United Kingdom	46,900	240,658	33,372	327,283	49,924	25,125	24,556	204,002	23,676

1 Includes age not reported.
2 Includes road user type not known.

3 Number of casualties: by county, by type of road user: 1981-85 average[1]

	Children (0-15)	Adults (16-59)	Older adults (60+)	All[2] casualties	Pedest-rians	Pedal cyclists	Motor cyclists	Car occupants	Other[3] road users
Avon	616	3,520	447	4,584	777	402	1,399	1,768	238
Bedfordshire	502	2,480	252	3,235	495	299	628	1,552	262
Berkshire	573	3,232	333	4,243	567	449	904	2,167	157
Buckinghamshire	464	2,713	283	3,504	409	287	700	1,940	168
Cambridgeshire	489	3,095	397	3,981	345	646	923	1,834	233
Cheshire	803	3,789	490	5,095	711	593	1,126	2,324	341
Cleveland	587	1,853	231	2,671	682	274	515	1,016	185
Cornwall	359	2,079	253	2,691	339	151	756	1,301	144
Cumbria	441	2,068	297	2,806	444	216	606	1,383	157
Derbyshire	715	3,505	439	4,933	808	405	1,207	2,098	415
Devon	769	4,333	624	5,726	845	400	1,654	2,526	302
Dorset	461	2,745	471	3,677	487	396	959	1,647	188
Durham	450	1,806	221	2,476	510	140	412	1,216	198
East Sussex	535	2,722	655	3,911	725	287	830	1,842	227
Essex	1,344	7,165	947	9,474	1,212	803	1,845	5,003	611
Gloucestershire	419	2,549	308	3,276	378	348	926	1,465	160
Greater London	7,106	37,831	5,855	54,156	13,081	4,739	9,957	21,778	4,601
Greater Manchester	2,946	9,320	1,431	13,699	3,931	1,376	2,284	5,186	922
Hampshire	1,276	7,151	881	9,308	1,159	1,182	2,530	3,981	456
Hereford & Worcester	491	2,895	384	3,770	461	370	847	1,909	183
Hertfordshire	784	4,401	485	5,729	738	511	1,173	3,003	304
Humberside	842	3,601	491	4,934	821	727	1,377	1,620	388
Isle of Wight	107	481	74	662	107	61	206	260	28
Kent	1,251	6,769	848	8,867	1,246	744	2,291	4,139	447
Lancashire	1,399	5,155	906	7,460	1,683	666	1,458	3,188	466
Leicestershire	752	3,657	415	4,825	827	507	1,117	2,124	249
Lincolnshire	501	2,866	382	3,749	365	381	852	1,929	221
Merseyside	1,632	4,718	875	7,225	2,066	583	1,009	2,926	642
Norfolk	551	3,195	495	4,241	483	456	1,063	1,999	240
Northamptonshire	499	2,818	334	3,652	449	240	779	1,913	271
Northumberland	215	1,142	159	1,516	192	95	270	828	131
North Yorkshire	568	3,349	496	4,413	531	420	1,030	2,150	283
Nottinghamshire	987	4,364	570	5,920	1,111	609	1,362	2,381	458
Oxfordshire	389	2,677	297	3,424	362	382	798	1,663	219
Shropshire	297	1,767	211	2,275	252	185	473	1,237	129
Somerset	299	1,875	276	2,450	267	222	640	1,204	117
South Yorkshire	1,108	4,121	685	5,914	1,475	354	1,069	2,308	708
Staffordshire	1,038	4,972	518	6,528	983	558	1,388	3,167	432
Suffolk	479	2,762	385	3,627	397	389	961	1,696	183
Surrey	921	5,844	779	7,640	808	838	1,764	3,918	312
Tyne & Wear	1,028	2,906	509	4,443	1,491	334	650	1,568	400
Warwickshire	400	2,179	261	2,839	339	295	606	1,446	154
West Midlands	2,714	8,345	1,227	12,286	3,596	1,064	1,993	4,812	820
West Sussex	498	2,919	527	3,943	440	464	907	1,953	180
West Yorkshire	2,039	7,531	1,084	10,654	2,728	722	2,048	4,386	770
Wiltshire	491	3,080	377	3,948	392	358	887	2,056	256
England	43,133	204,343	28,867	280,382	52,515	25,927	59,179	123,806	18,956
Wales	2,320	10,500	1,576	14,395	2,666	857	2,566	7,211	1,094
Scotland	4,881	19,157	3,097	27,134	6,560	1,607	3,446	12,924	2,598
Great Britain	50,334	234,000	33,540	321,912	61,741	28,391	65,191	143,941	22,647
Northern Ireland[4]	1,516	5,954	731	8,204	1,648	399	765	5,398	
United Kingdom[4]	51,850	239,954	34,271	330,115	63,389	28,791	65,956	171,986	

1 Figures have been rounded so there may be an apparent slight discrepancy between the sum of the constituent items and the total as shown.
2 Includes age not reported.
3 Includes road user type not known.
4 It is not possible to give separate casualty figures for car occupants and other road users for Northern Ireland for these years.

4 Total casualty rates[1] : by county, by type of road user: 1994

Rate per 100,000 population

	Children (0-15)	Adults (16-59)	Elderly (60+)	All[2] casualties	Pedest- rians	Pedal cyclists	Motor cyclists	Car occupants	Other[3] road users
Avon	253	460	172	366	55	32	37	216	25
Bedfordshire	329	664	256	520	66	39	38	343	35
Berkshire	301	622	244	512	58	45	45	342	22
Buckinghamshire	321	715	306	581	52	39	46	413	31
Cambridgeshire	333	809	364	640	46	102	61	398	33
Cheshire	380	866	309	653	64	43	44	451	52
Cleveland	419	568	258	475	104	40	17	285	28
Cornwall	388	775	311	583	65	31	65	379	43
Cumbria	354	687	278	529	67	35	49	343	35
Derbyshire	345	665	246	536	73	34	49	356	24
Devon	331	643	231	480	71	35	56	298	20
Dorset	334	723	271	527	53	46	50	348	31
Durham	343	538	208	429	75	19	21	274	40
East Sussex	424	755	335	580	94	46	48	346	46
Essex	364	768	293	609	66	46	45	417	35
Gloucestershire	290	672	284	510	50	44	49	340	26
Greater London	390	768	325	661	138	64	79	326	54
Greater Manchester	519	825	293	654	124	46	24	413	48
Hampshire	359	717	276	556	61	65	54	347	30
Hereford & Worcester	321	667	273	513	59	41	43	329	40
Hertfordshire	324	766	267	583	53	41	45	417	28
Humberside	442	699	248	550	88	78	55	284	45
Isle of Wight	411	678	261	507	74	59	68	277	30
Kent	363	681	259	532	64	45	56	340	27
Lancashire	493	829	328	653	101	43	35	421	52
Leicestershire	350	659	259	522	74	47	40	327	35
Lincolnshire	399	776	288	586	51	50	54	385	46
Merseyside	545	898	341	704	117	40	24	470	54
Norfolk	401	719	279	574	53	47	53	389	32
Northamptonshire	301	661	285	516	60	33	37	359	27
Northumberland	400	595	266	483	55	30	27	327	44
North Yorkshire	431	859	325	656	59	49	56	445	48
Nottinghamshire	432	673	265	578	86	49	46	348	49
Oxfordshire	309	651	268	532	43	59	46	348	36
Shropshire	309	689	277	525	52	33	43	362	34
Somerset	313	655	264	506	47	39	40	356	22
South Yorkshire	446	570	227	473	88	32	27	283	43
Staffordshire	458	806	298	660	78	42	47	441	53
Suffolk	299	575	235	441	45	46	49	275	26
Surrey	376	912	331	729	61	60	66	510	32
Tyne & Wear	398	501	207	417	98	29	13	245	32
Warwickshire	379	838	295	665	66	50	49	454	45
West Midlands	393	570	221	461	105	36	25	268	27
West Sussex	339	707	254	519	47	54	45	344	29
West Yorkshire	424	682	285	549	111	30	27	342	38
Wiltshire	314	747	321	573	48	46	53	387	40
England	390	715	280	572	86	47	46	354	39
Wales	81	667	264	520	76	27	30	348	39
Scotland	404	521	242	441	92	27	18	259	44
Great Britain	391	695	276	557	86	44	43	345	39
Northern Ireland	418	999	361	741	78	19	15	545	84
United Kingdom	392	703	278	562	86	43	42	351	41

1 Based on final 1993 population estimates.
2 Includes age not reported.
3 Includes road user type not known.

5 Casualty indicators: by county, by type of road user: 1994

	Percentage of all casualties who are:				Percentage of all casualties			
	Children[1] (0-15)	Adults[1] (16-59)	Elderly[1] (60+)	Pedest-rians	Pedal cyclists	Motor cyclists	Car occupants	Other[2] road users
Avon	13.7	76.2	10.2	15.0	8.8	10.2	59.1	6.9
Bedfordshire	14.1	77.5	8.3	12.7	7.4	7.3	65.9	6.7
Berkshire	13.1	78.7	8.3	11.4	8.8	8.8	66.7	4.3
Buckinghamshire	12.6	78.2	9.2	9.0	6.6	7.8	71.1	5.4
Cambridgeshire	10.9	78.4	10.8	7.2	16.0	9.5	62.2	5.2
Cheshire	12.1	78.4	9.4	9.8	6.6	6.7	69.0	7.9
Cleveland	20.0	69.5	10.4	21.9	8.5	3.6	60.2	5.8
Cornwall	12.9	73.4	13.7	11.1	5.4	11.1	65.0	7.4
Cumbria	13.1	74.8	12.1	12.7	6.6	9.2	64.9	6.6
Derbyshire	13.5	76.3	10.2	13.6	6.4	9.1	66.4	4.5
Devon	12.9	74.9	12.2	14.7	7.4	11.7	62.0	4.2
Dorset	11.3	74.4	14.4	10.0	8.7	9.5	66.0	5.8
Durham	16.3	73.4	10.3	17.5	4.5	4.8	64.0	9.3
East Sussex	13.1	71.0	15.9	16.2	7.9	8.2	59.7	8.0
Essex	12.5	76.9	10.6	10.8	7.6	7.3	68.5	5.7
Gloucestershire	11.3	76.3	12.4	9.8	8.7	9.6	66.8	5.2
Greater London	12.8	77.6	9.6	20.9	9.6	12.0	49.3	8.1
Greater Manchester	17.2	74.0	8.8	18.9	7.0	3.7	63.2	7.3
Hampshire	13.1	76.9	10.0	11.0	11.7	9.6	62.4	5.3
Hereford & Worcester	12.7	75.8	11.4	11.6	7.9	8.5	64.2	7.8
Hertfordshire	11.6	79.4	9.0	9.0	7.0	7.7	71.5	4.8
Humberside	16.8	73.6	9.6	16.0	14.2	10.0	51.6	8.2
Isle of Wight	14.8	70.1	15.0	14.5	11.5	13.4	54.5	6.0
Kent	14.2	75.2	10.6	12.1	8.4	10.5	63.9	5.1
Lancashire	15.9	73.1	11.0	15.5	6.6	5.4	64.5	7.9
Leicestershire	14.3	76.0	9.7	14.1	9.0	7.6	62.5	6.7
Lincolnshire	13.1	75.1	11.8	8.7	8.5	9.1	65.8	7.9
Merseyside	16.5	73.2	10.3	16.7	5.6	3.4	66.7	7.6
Norfolk	13.6	73.9	12.5	9.2	8.2	9.2	67.7	5.7
Northamptonshire	13.6	76.0	10.4	11.6	6.5	7.2	69.6	5.1
Northumberland	16.5	71.2	12.3	11.5	6.1	5.7	67.7	9.1
North Yorkshire	12.6	76.0	11.5	9.0	7.5	8.5	67.8	7.2
Nottinghamshire	16.2	73.8	10.0	14.9	8.5	8.0	60.1	8.4
Oxfordshire	12.3	78.1	9.6	8.1	11.0	8.7	65.4	6.8
Shropshire	12.1	76.9	11.0	9.9	6.3	8.2	69.0	6.5
Somerset	12.7	74.1	13.2	9.4	7.8	8.0	70.5	4.4
South Yorkshire	19.0	71.0	10.0	18.7	6.7	5.8	59.8	9.1
Staffordshire	14.8	76.0	9.2	11.7	6.3	7.2	66.7	8.0
Suffolk	13.9	73.9	12.1	10.2	10.4	11.1	62.4	5.9
Surrey	10.6	79.1	10.3	8.4	8.3	9.1	69.9	4.4
Tyne & Wear	19.4	70.0	10.6	23.6	7.0	3.1	58.7	7.6
Warwickshire	11.8	78.5	9.6	9.9	7.6	7.4	68.3	6.8
West Midlands	18.6	71.7	9.7	22.9	7.7	5.3	58.2	5.9
West Sussex	12.4	74.8	12.8	9.0	10.5	8.6	66.2	5.6
West Yorkshire	16.5	73.3	10.2	20.3	5.5	4.9	62.4	6.9
Wiltshire	11.3	77.4	11.2	8.4	8.0	9.2	67.5	7.0
England	14.2	75.4	10.4	15.0	8.2	8.1	61.9	6.8
Wales	15.6	72.9	11.4	14.6	5.3	5.7	67.0	7.5
Scotland	18.4	70.4	11.1	21.0	6.1	4.1	58.8	10.0
Great Britain	14.6	74.9	10.5	15.4	7.9	7.7	61.9	7.1
Northern Ireland	14.5	77.2	8.3	10.5	2.6	2.0	73.5	11.3
United Kingdom	14.3	73.5	10.2	15.3	7.7	7.5	62.3	7.2

1 Percentage of casualties of known age.
2 Includes road user type not known.

22

6 Casualty changes: by county and severity: 1981-85 average, 1994

	Fatal and serious casualties			Total casualties		
	1981-85 average	1994	percentage change	1981-85 average	1994	percentage change
Avon	1,356	467	-65.6	4,584	3,561	-22.3
Bedfordshire	714	421	-41.1	3,235	2,806	-13.3
Berkshire	1,095	393	-64.1	4,243	3,911	-7.8
Buckinghamshire	1,031	398	-61.4	3,504	3,785	8.0
Cambridgeshire	1,087	837	-23.0	3,981	4,368	9.7
Cheshire	916	1,073	17.1	5,095	6,349	24.6
Cleveland	486	270	-44.5	2,671	2,655	-0.6
Cornwall	858	468	-45.4	2,691	2,781	3.4
Cumbria	829	539	-35.0	2,806	2,591	-7.7
Derbyshire	1,222	563	-53.9	4,933	5,097	3.3
Devon	1,897	791	-58.3	5,726	5,040	-12.0
Dorset	940	462	-50.9	3,677	3,518	-4.3
Durham	703	366	-48.0	2,476	2,604	5.2
East Sussex	989	656	-33.7	3,911	4,187	7.0
Essex	2,398	1,487	-38.0	9,474	9,505	0.3
Gloucestershire	1,166	434	-62.8	3,276	2,772	-15.4
Greater London[1]	8,230 (9,175)	6,195	-24.7	54,156	45,837	-15.4
Greater Manchester	2,362	1,526	-35.4	13,699	16,872	23.2
Hampshire	2,755	1,401	-49.2	9,308	8,859	-4.8
Hereford & Worcester	1,071	866	-19.2	3,770	3,562	-5.5
Hertfordshire	1,388	931	-32.9	5,729	5,830	1.8
Humberside	1,129	852	-24.5	4,934	4,863	-1.4
Isle of Wight	184	120	-34.8	662	633	-4.4
Kent	2,385	1,407	-41.0	8,867	8,192	-7.6
Lancashire	1,704	1,754	2.9	7,460	9,273	24.3
Leicestershire	1,226	611	-50.2	4,825	4,755	-1.4
Lincolnshire	1,074	766	-28.7	3,749	3,525	-6.0
Merseyside	1,237	923	-25.4	7,225	10,151	40.5
Norfolk	1,524	1,033	-32.2	4,241	4,389	3.5
Northamptonshire	1,328	778	-41.4	3,652	3,056	-16.3
Northumberland	400	293	-26.7	1,516	1,484	-2.1
North Yorkshire	1,835	1,264	-31.1	4,413	4,734	7.3
Nottinghamshire	1,540	1,187	-22.9	5,920	5,942	0.4
Oxfordshire	1,067	418	-60.8	3,424	3,118	-8.9
Shropshire	833	622	-25.3	2,275	2,173	-4.5
Somerset	811	411	-49.3	2,450	2,398	-2.1
South Yorkshire	1,320	715	-45.8	5,914	6,185	4.6
Staffordshire	1,442	809	-43.9	6,528	6,957	6.6
Suffolk	1,170	533	-54.4	3,627	2,851	-21.4
Surrey	1,641	925	-43.6	7,640	7,567	-1.0
Tyne & Wear	1,048	744	-29.0	4,443	4,748	6.9
Warwickshire	1,059	768	-27.5	2,839	3,282	15.6
West Midlands	3,452	2,238	-35.2	12,286	12,140	-1.2
West Sussex	922	587	-36.3	3,943	3,724	-5.6
West Yorkshire	2,547	1,526	-40.1	10,654	11,528	8.2
Wiltshire	1,019	575	-43.6	3,948	3,343	-15.3
England	67,388	42,403	-37.1	280,382	277,501	-1.0
Wales	3,855	2,208	-42.7	14,395	15,105	4.9
Scotland	8,887	5,570	-37.3	27,134	22,583	-16.8
Great Britain	80,130	50,181	-37.4	321,912	315,189	-2.1
Northern Ireland	2,362	1,805	-23.6	8,204	12,094	47.4
United Kingdom	82,492	51,986	-37.0	330,115	327,283	-0.9

1 In September 1984 the Metropolitan Police implemented revised standards in the assessment of serious casualties.
   Figures in brackets estimate casualty totals under standards prevailing since 1984. See preface.

7 Number of casualties: by road class, region[1] and severity: 1994

	Motorways	Built up				Non built up				All roads[2]
		Trunk	Principal	Other	Total	Trunk	Principal	Other	Total	
Northern[3]										
Killed	6	3	29	50	82	24	42	24	90	178
Killed or Seriously Injured	45	32	400	863	1,295	225	367	280	872	2,212
All Casualties	247	227	2,990	5,962	9,179	1,326	1,882	1,448	4,656	14,082
Yorkshire and Humberside										
Killed	10	5	83	71	159	30	73	53	156	325
Killed or Seriously Injured	67	73	935	1,640	2,648	397	616	629	1,642	4,357
All Casualties	895	589	7,243	11,896	19,728	1,610	2,677	2,400	6,687	27,310
East Midlands										
Killed	4	16	47	69	132	57	83	65	205	341
Killed or Seriously Injured	107	129	649	1,188	1,966	470	727	635	1,832	3,905
All Casualties	730	922	4,502	7,907	13,331	2,189	3,190	2,935	8,314	22,375
Eastern										
Killed	27	7	45	70	122	77	123	89	289	438
Killed or Seriously Injured	191	88	797	1,693	2,578	612	1,002	1,257	2,871	5,640
All Casualties	1,628	608	5,894	11,465	17,967	3,173	5,021	5,739	13,933	33,534
South East										
Killed	17	9	83	81	173	50	117	70	237	427
Killed or Seriously Injured	252	104	1,241	1,865	3,210	420	1,074	951	2,445	5,907
All Casualties	2,302	722	9,365	13,843	23,930	2,444	6,040	5,475	13,959	40,191
Greater London										
Killed	6	36	138	81	255	7	2	0	9	270
Killed or Seriously Injured	96	589	3,069	2,235	5,893	131	40	35	206	6,195
All Casualties	684	4,543	22,467	16,667	43,677	958	319	199	1,476	45,837
South West										
Killed	15	1	34	45	80	62	115	56	233	336
Killed or Seriously Injured	114	28	490	1,072	1,590	310	864	721	1,895	3,608
All Casualties	762	300	4,355	7,981	12,636	1,630	4,325	4,047	10,002	23,413
West Midlands										
Killed	18	10	89	79	178	60	93	33	186	382
Killed or Seriously Injured	221	109	1,288	1,988	3,385	429	661	607	1,697	5,303
All Casualties	1,325	756	7,982	11,142	19,880	1,754	2,461	2,694	6,909	28,114
North West[3]										
Killed	32	8	100	123	231	35	58	24	117	380
Killed or Seriously Injured	260	106	1,538	2,286	3,930	275	467	344	1,086	5,276
All Casualties	2,394	1,026	15,007	18,537	34,570	1,410	2,569	1,701	5,680	42,645
England										
Killed	135	95	648	669	1,412	402	706	414	1,522	3,077
Killed or Seriously Injured	1,353	1,258	10,407	14,830	26,495	3,269	5,818	5,459	14,546	42,403
All Casualties	10,967	9,693	79,805	105,400	194,898	16,494	28,484	26,638	71,616	277,501
Wales										
Killed	6	9	33	46	88	44	48	24	116	210
Killed or Seriously Injured	33	81	369	660	1,110	382	369	314	1,065	2,208
All Casualties	271	513	2,895	5,922	9,330	1,945	1,888	1,670	5,503	15,105
Scotland										
Killed	16	8	41	62	111	99	91	46	236	363
Killed or Seriously Injured	129	121	936	1,938	2,995	816	925	705	2,446	5,570
All Casualties	512	527	4,529	8,924	13,980	2,580	3,073	2,438	8,091	22,583
Great Britain										
Killed	157	112	722	777	1,611	545	845	484	1,874	3,650
Killed or Seriously Injured	1,515	1,460	11,712	17,428	30,600	4,467	7,112	6,478	18,057	50,181
All Casualties	11,750	10,733	87,229	120,246	218,208	21,019	33,445	30,746	85,210	315,189

1 Casualty data by road class are not available for Northern Ireland.
2 Includes speed limit not reported.
3 From 1st April 1991 responsibilty for Cumbria transferred from the North West Regional Office to the Northern Regional Office.
  The change to the road accident database was deferred until 1992. Consequently data prior to 1992 for both Northern and North West regions shown in
  this table in previous editions of RASER are not comparable with the 1994 data presented above.

8 Casualty rates per 100 million vehicle kilometres: by road class, region[1] and severity: 1992-1994 average

Rate per 100 million vehicle kilometres[2]

	Motorways	A roads Built up Trunk	A roads Built up Principal	A roads Non built up Trunk	A roads Non built up Principal	All A roads	All major roads[3]
Northern[4]							
Fatal	1.0	1.9	1.2	1.5	1.5	1.4	1.4
Fatal or serious	5.6	45.2	17.0	8.9	11.8	12.6	12.0
All severities	34.8	337.6	122.3	49.8	60.6	76.9	73.2
Yorkshire and Humberside							
Fatal	0.3	1.1	1.4	0.8	2.0	1.4	1.1
Fatal or serious	2.1	12.6	16.1	9.0	16.7	14.0	11.2
All severities	17.5	92.4	110.5	34.2	64.6	75.4	61.7
East Midlands							
Fatal	0.3	1.5	1.2	1.1	1.6	1.3	1.1
Fatal or serious	2.9	14.3	16.9	7.6	14.6	12.4	10.6
All severities	18.1	95.6	116.1	34.9	63.5	66.6	57.1
Eastern							
Fatal	0.4	0.8	1.0	0.9	1.6	1.1	1.0
Fatal or serious	3.3	13.2	16.8	6.6	13.3	11.2	9.5
All severities	25.3	97.3	120.1	32.2	63.1	63.0	54.8
South East							
Fatal	0.2	1.5	0.8	0.6	1.0	0.8	0.6
Fatal or serious	1.8	16.9	12.9	4.8	8.8	9.2	6.7
All severities	13.8	116.5	93.3	27.9	47.1	57.9	42.9
Greater London							
Fatal	0.2	1.3	1.3	0.4	0.6	1.1	1.1
Fatal or serious	4.8	19.8	30.1	6.3	11.4	24.2	22.4
All severities	37.8	144.5	209.5	38.7	78.7	168.8	156.4
South West							
Fatal	0.3	0.7	0.8	1.0	1.4	1.1	0.9
Fatal or serious	1.9	11.0	10.6	5.8	11.0	9.4	7.8
All severities	12.3	97.1	74.8	30.2	53.1	53.8	44.7
West Midlands							
Fatal	0.3	1.3	1.3	1.4	1.6	1.4	1.1
Fatal or serious	2.7	12.6	17.7	10.0	12.3	14.1	10.2
All severities	15.5	90.8	111.7	42.7	54.5	77.6	56.5
North West[4]							
Fatal	0.3	0.9	1.2	0.7	1.2	1.1	0.8
Fatal or serious	2.0	11.0	14.7	5.7	8.7	11.4	8.0
All severities	18.7	115.3	138.3	34.8	51.3	96.6	68.7
England							
Fatal	0.3	1.2	1.1	0.9	1.4	1.2	0.9
Fatal or serious	2.4	16.1	17.6	6.9	11.6	12.7	10.0
All severities	17.7	120.0	128.5	34.2	55.8	79.3	63.3
Wales							
Fatal	0.2	1.1	1.1	1.1	1.3	1.2	1.0
Fatal or serious	1.6	11.0	12.7	9.5	12.3	11.2	9.9
All severities	13.8	69.5	96.4	43.3	58.6	63.6	56.5
Scotland							
Fatal	0.5	1.2	0.9	1.5	1.6	1.3	1.2
Fatal or serious	3.2	15.7	16.3	11.2	15.2	14.1	12.4
All severities	14.4	72.9	83.9	36.8	53.6	56.8	50.3
Great Britain							
Fatal	0.3	1.2	1.1	1.0	1.4	1.2	1.0
Fatal or serious	2.4	15.7	17.3	7.6	12.0	12.7	10.2
All severities	17.4	111.9	123.6	35.2	55.7	76.2	61.8

1 Casualty and traffic data by road class are not available for Northern Ireland.
2 Traffic for 1992 has been revised.
3 Includes road class and type not reported.
4 From 1st April 1991 responsibilty for Cumbria transferred from the North West Regional Office to the Northern Regional Office.
  The change to the road accident database was deferred until 1992.

9 Accident rates per 100 million vehicle kilometres: by road class, region[1] and severity: 1992-1994 average

Rate per 100 million vehicle kilometres[2]

| | Motorways | A roads | | | | All A roads | All major roads[3] |
| | | Built up | | Non built up | | | |
		Trunk	Principal	Trunk	Principal		
Northern[4]							
Fatal	0.9	1.4	1.2	1.3	1.3	1.3	1.3
Fatal or serious	4.2	41.4	15.8	6.4	8.8	10.3	9.7
All severities	22.2	245.7	93.7	28.6	36.6	52.0	49.3
Yorkshire and Humberside							
Fatal	0.3	1.0	1.3	0.7	1.6	1.2	1.0
Fatal or serious	1.6	11.6	14.3	6.1	11.6	11.1	8.9
All severities	10.9	70.1	84.2	19.7	38.6	52.7	42.8
East Midlands							
Fatal	0.3	1.4	1.1	1.0	1.4	1.2	1.0
Fatal or serious	2.0	12.6	15.1	5.7	10.7	9.9	8.3
All severities	10.5	72.3	88.7	20.9	39.3	45.6	38.8
Eastern							
Fatal	0.4	0.7	0.9	0.7	1.4	1.0	0.9
Fatal or serious	2.5	11.3	15.3	5.0	9.7	8.9	7.5
All severities	15.9	73.1	93.6	19.7	40.7	43.9	37.8
South East							
Fatal	0.2	1.5	0.8	0.6	0.9	0.8	0.6
Fatal or serious	1.3	13.8	11.8	3.7	6.8	7.7	5.5
All severities	8.5	85.4	74.0	17.5	30.7	42.0	30.5
Greater London							
Fatal	0.2	1.3	1.3	0.4	0.6	1.1	1.0
Fatal or serious	3.7	17.2	27.6	5.3	9.4	21.9	20.2
All severities	27.3	116.2	177.8	27.9	59.4	141.2	130.4
South West							
Fatal	0.2	0.7	0.7	0.9	1.2	0.9	0.8
Fatal or serious	1.4	10.0	9.4	4.2	8.3	7.5	6.2
All severities	7.4	77.8	59.5	18.8	33.7	37.7	31.1
West Midlands							
Fatal	0.2	1.3	1.2	1.2	1.4	1.3	0.9
Fatal or serious	1.9	10.9	15.4	7.2	9.2	11.4	8.2
All severities	9.3	68.0	84.7	26.8	35.2	55.7	39.9
North West[4]							
Fatal	0.3	0.8	1.2	0.6	1.0	1.0	0.7
Fatal or serious	1.5	9.6	13.3	4.1	6.5	9.8	6.8
All severities	11.4	79.8	99.8	20.9	31.6	67.4	47.4
England							
Fatal	0.2	1.2	1.1	0.8	1.2	1.0	0.8
Fatal or serious	1.7	14.0	15.9	5.1	8.6	10.5	8.3
All severities	10.9	92.6	101.0	21.0	35.3	58.0	45.7
Wales							
Fatal	0.2	1.0	1.0	0.9	1.2	1.0	0.9
Fatal or serious	1.3	9.1	10.6	6.4	9.0	8.4	7.4
All severities	8.9	50.6	69.3	24.5	35.1	41.2	36.6
Scotland							
Fatal	0.4	1.2	0.9	1.2	1.4	1.2	1.1
Fatal or serious	2.5	13.5	14.9	7.6	11.0	11.0	9.7
All severities	9.2	54.3	67.6	21.8	33.7	39.8	35.1
Great Britain							
Fatal	0.3	1.2	1.1	0.9	1.2	1.1	0.9
Fatal or serious	1.8	13.6	15.6	5.5	8.9	10.5	8.3
All severities	10.8	85.9	97.0	21.4	35.1	55.2	44.3

1 Accident and traffic data by road class are not available for Northern Ireland.
2 Traffic for 1992 has been revised.
3 Includes road class and type not reported.
4 From 1st April 1991 responsibilty for Cumbria transferred from the North West Regional Office to the Northern Regional Office. This change to road accident database was deferred until 1992.

10 Accident indices[1]: by month, severity and region: accidents by severity and region: 1994

Index/ number

	Jan	Feb	Mar	Apr	May	Jun	Jul	Aug	Sep	Oct	Nov	Dec	All accidents
Northern[2]													
Fatal & serious	96	100	96	93	98	92	103	90	119	95	117	101	1,913
All	89	98	91	89	92	98	100	94	105	113	120	111	10,124
Yorkshire and Humberside													
Fatal & serious	106	86	79	91	96	103	106	91	99	103	120	120	3,627
All	92	96	92	93	90	91	103	94	105	110	115	119	20,121
East Midlands													
Fatal & serious	99	100	94	85	89	102	96	99	95	104	113	122	3,231
All	97	99	92	89	90	97	95	94	105	112	112	119	16,091
Eastern													
Fatal & serious	106	86	90	88	97	95	109	94	97	105	115	115	4,715
All	102	101	91	90	100	95	93	94	98	109	107	118	24,260
South East													
Fatal & serious	96	88	92	96	92	100	101	101	98	111	110	114	5,087
All	98	97	91	91	96	100	98	97	100	112	110	109	29,824
Greater London													
Fatal & serious	112	94	93	87	91	108	105	100	108	119	102	81	5,659
All	100	93	99	99	99	105	99	94	102	111	102	96	38,527
South West													
Fatal & serious	90	93	94	92	92	108	99	98	110	111	105	108	3,017
All	93	100	90	89	97	102	102	106	102	110	108	101	17,150
West Midlands													
Fatal & serious	95	101	99	103	91	100	101	98	96	96	107	112	4,420
All	94	98	90	94	94	101	99	93	100	109	113	114	20,571
North West[2]													
Fatal & serious	96	87	90	100	98	97	102	98	88	112	110	119	4,525
All	96	92	96	96	91	97	99	93	104	113	111	111	30,120
England													
Fatal & serious	100	92	92	93	94	101	103	97	100	107	110	110	36,194
All	97	96	93	93	95	99	98	95	102	111	110	110	206,788
Wales													
Fatal & serious	93	95	78	82	94	114	105	122	99	116	112	90	1,776
All	98	97	97	90	93	98	110	105	99	106	107	99	10,536
Scotland													
Fatal & serious	90	93	100	88	76	95	95	106	109	115	111	121	4,642
All	94	100	107	96	82	100	94	107	94	105	107	112	16,777
Great Britain													
Fatal & serious	99	92	92	92	92	101	102	99	101	109	110	110	42,612
All	97	97	94	93	94	99	99	97	101	110	110	109	234,101
Northern Ireland													
Fatal & serious	101	92	120	85	100	103	89	102	87	108	98	113	1,324
All	107	94	109	92	88	102	83	96	101	96	121	110	6,682
United Kingdom													
Fatal & serious	99	92	93	92	92	101	102	99	100	109	110	110	43,936
All	97	97	95	93	94	99	98	97	101	110	110	109	240,783

1 The base(=100) is the average number of accidents per day for the region.
2 From 1st April 1991 responsibilty for Cumbria transferred from the North West Regional Office to the Northern Regional Office.
   The change to the road accident database was deferred until 1992. Consequently data prior to 1992 for both Northern and North West regions shown in
   this table in previous editions of RASER are not comparable with the 1994 data presented above.

11 Accidents on motorways: by carriageway type, junction, number of lanes, region[1] and severity: 1994

Number of accidents

	Junction			Non-junction		
	Number of lanes		Circular section of roundabouts	Number of lanes		Total[2]
	2	3+		2	3+	
Northern[3]						
Fatal or serious	5	1	0	6	16	31
All severities	26	8	11	44	59	168
Yorkshire and Humberside						
Fatal or serious	3	2	2	4	44	56
All severities	29	16	82	43	366	559
East Midlands						
Fatal or serious	0	3	2	3	63	72
All severities	6	21	20	17	329	428
Eastern						
Fatal or serious	1	13	2	12	103	140
All severities	30	97	17	96	713	1,020
South East						
Fatal or serious	7	9	5	34	129	191
All severities	53	90	73	149	946	1,430
London						
Fatal or serious	8	13	1	14	36	75
All severities	67	99	9	74	261	527
of which:						
Inner London						
Fatal or serious	2	0	0	5	3	12
All severities	15	17	4	12	18	75
Outer London						
Fatal or serious	6	13	1	9	33	63
All severities	52	82	5	62	243	452
South West						
Fatal or serious	1	2	0	6	63	79
All severities	11	33	15	41	293	427
West Midlands						
Fatal or serious	3	14	1	16	125	168
All severities	11	54	10	51	609	789
North West[3]						
Fatal or serious	2	11	6	14	104	181
All severities	62	104	99	112	735	1,368
England						
Fatal or serious	30	68	19	109	683	993
All severities	295	522	336	627	4,311	6,716
Wales						
Fatal or serious	4	0	1	12	6	26
All severities	16	2	25	55	70	179
Scotland						
Fatal or serious	6	8	0	40	30	99
All severities	28	23	8	121	107	330
Great Britain						
Fatal or serious	40	76	20	161	719	1,118
All severities	339	547	369	803	4,488	7,225

1 Accident data by road class are not available for Northern Ireland.
2 Includes unknown carriageway type and slip roads.
3 From 1st April 1991 responsibilty for Cumbria transferred from the North West Regional Office to the Northern Regional Office.
  The change to the road accident database was deferred until 1992. Consequently data prior to 1992 for both Northern and North West regions
  shown in this table in previous editions of RASER are not comparable with the 1994 data presented above.

12 Accidents on trunk 'A' roads: by carriageway type, junction, number of lanes, region[1] and severity: 1994

Number of accidents

	Dual carriageway					Single carriageway							Circular section of round-about[5]	All trunk A roads[6]
	Junction		Non-junction			Junction			Non-junction					
	Number of lanes[2]		Number of lanes[2]			Number of lanes[3]			Number of lanes[3]					
	2	3+	2	3+	All	2[4]	3	4+	2[4]	3	4+	All		
Northern[7]														
Fatal or serious	33	3	33	1	70	44	3	1	67	2	0	117	10	197
All severities	143	14	212	25	394	220	6	2	193	5	0	426	81	906
Yorkshire and Humberside														
Fatal or serious	57	4	66	6	133	82	7	4	93	2	3	191	15	339
All severities	157	23	266	17	463	373	25	25	320	5	8	756	149	1,378
East Midlands														
Fatal or serious	45	2	71	6	124	122	11	17	144	1	6	301	35	461
All severities	201	11	308	19	539	575	44	69	482	7	30	1,207	275	2,026
Eastern														
Fatal or serious	95	8	120	14	237	114	7	3	148	3	2	277	34	549
All severities	338	38	532	65	973	521	38	7	532	7	6	1,111	303	2,398
South East														
Fatal or serious	49	15	96	32	192	67	8	2	91	0	1	169	29	395
All severities	244	82	455	148	929	384	24	17	348	6	9	788	293	2,034
London														
Fatal or serious	74	101	52	70	297	186	8	35	49	4	20	302	33	637
All severities	548	730	325	446	2,049	1,244	62	259	332	19	75	1,991	293	4,406
of which:														
Inner London														
Fatal or serious	26	34	12	17	89	110	5	25	23	1	11	175	4	272
All severities	171	252	53	89	565	676	28	174	148	7	38	1,071	33	1,701
Outer London														
Fatal or serious	48	67	40	53	208	76	3	10	26	3	9	127	29	365
All severities	377	478	272	357	1,484	568	34	85	184	12	37	920	260	2,705
South West														
Fatal or serious	22	4	40	1	67	51	3	1	103	13	1	172	10	251
All severities	87	22	193	16	318	315	23	8	382	48	2	778	143	1,249
West Midlands														
Fatal or serious	59	9	62	1	131	95	4	2	132	3	0	236	23	391
All severities	250	36	242	14	542	432	36	8	362	14	0	852	224	1,623
North West[7]														
Fatal or serious	41	30	27	7	105	70	7	12	57	2	10	158	17	280
All severities	261	147	128	30	566	402	32	79	220	8	38	779	161	1,519
England														
Fatal or serious	475	176	567	138	1,356	831	58	77	884	30	43	1,923	206	3,500
All severities	2,229	1,103	2,661	780	6,773	4,466	290	474	3,171	119	168	8,688	1,922	17,539
Wales														
Fatal or serious	16	1	43	0	60	78	9	1	162	8	0	258	11	329
All severities	100	11	225	7	343	409	27	3	581	37	0	1,057	79	1,487
Scotland														
Fatal or serious	62	6	82	10	160	125	7	0	312	3	10	457	10	631
All severities	182	14	286	26	508	429	16	7	841	10	20	1,323	50	1,894
Great Britain														
Fatal or serious	553	183	692	148	1,576	1,034	74	78	1,358	41	53	2,638	227	4,460
All severities	2,511	1,128	3,172	813	7,624	5,304	333	484	4,593	166	188	11,068	2,051	20,920

1 Accident data by road class are not available for Northern Ireland.
2 Number of lanes in each direction.
3 Number of lanes in both directions.
4 Includes one way streets.
5 These are classified as junction accidents.
6 Includes unknown carriageway type and single track roads.
7 From 1st April 1991 responsibilty for Cumbria transferred from the North West Regional Office to the Northern Regional Office. The change to the road accident database was deferred until 1992. Consequently data prior to 1992 for both Northern and North West regions shown in this table in previous editions of RASER are not comparable with the 1994 data presented above.

13 Accidents on principal 'A' roads: by carriageway type, junction, number of lanes, region[1] and severity: 1994

Number of accidents

	Dual carriageway					Single carriageway							Circular section of round-about[5]	All principal A roads[6]
	Junction		Non-junction			Junction			Non-junction					
	Number of lanes[2]		Number of lanes[2]			Number of lanes[3]			Number of lanes[3]					
	2	3+	2	3+	All	2^4	3	4+	2^4	3	4+	All		
Northern[7]														
Fatal or serious	43	5	61	7	116	219	12	10	226	10	3	480	35	637
All severities	295	38	217	31	581	1,311	69	93	884	37	24	2,418	345	3,375
Yorkshire and Humberside														
Fatal or serious	93	20	82	14	209	488	37	14	445	10	3	997	49	1,258
All severities	653	188	326	62	1,229	3,078	181	117	1,732	55	35	5,198	589	7,055
East Midlands														
Fatal or serious	58	7	50	4	119	431	24	80	397	5	22	959	35	1,114
All severities	330	104	201	21	656	2,175	93	409	1,560	23	109	4,369	330	5,369
Eastern														
Fatal or serious	91	7	106	12	216	545	27	14	546	20	2	1,154	102	1,476
All severities	504	51	490	48	1,093	3,102	156	51	2,118	77	18	5,522	1,167	7,861
South East														
Fatal or serious	114	19	145	13	291	804	42	36	652	22	15	1,571	89	1,976
All severities	781	141	641	58	1,621	4,699	233	213	2,913	83	71	8,212	1,218	11,286
London														
Fatal or serious	209	44	101	18	372	1,550	54	224	478	12	72	2,390	66	2,857
All severities	1,391	322	497	101	2,311	10,658	352	1,586	3,016	80	396	16,088	687	19,368
of which:														
Inner London														
Fatal or serious	126	35	44	10	215	849	38	163	201	8	57	1,316	26	1,568
All severities	752	215	228	63	1,258	5,518	211	1,155	1,326	49	288	8,547	276	10,198
Outer London														
Fatal or serious	83	9	57	8	157	701	16	61	277	4	15	1,074	40	1,289
All severities	639	107	269	38	1,053	5,140	141	431	1,690	31	108	7,541	411	9,170
South West														
Fatal or serious	52	6	42	6	106	380	19	6	497	21	7	930	47	1,090
All severities	345	45	287	34	711	2,496	101	36	2,101	64	19	4,817	571	6,169
West Midlands														
Fatal or serious	170	45	133	20	368	564	19	37	481	14	19	1,134	73	1,584
All severities	868	246	474	67	1,655	3,127	133	167	1,731	36	58	5,252	592	7,543
North West[7]														
Fatal or serious	147	92	99	30	368	678	32	115	435	11	34	1,305	41	1,731
All severities	1,365	714	503	165	2,747	5,315	305	788	1,967	60	163	8,598	542	12,166
England														
Fatal or serious	977	245	819	124	2,165	5,659	266	536	4,157	125	177	10,920	537	13,723
All severities	6,532	1,849	3,636	587	12,604	35,961	1,623	3,460	18,022	515	893	60,474	6,041	80,192
Wales														
Fatal or serious	18	11	22	3	54	178	28	6	270	8	4	494	21	570
All severities	192	59	139	17	407	1,116	118	70	1,132	32	29	2,497	275	3,201
Scotland														
Fatal or serious	80	21	123	15	239	422	20	64	653	5	55	1,219	45	1,520
All severities	386	115	398	80	979	1,749	63	289	1,987	21	141	4,250	280	5,568
Great Britain														
Fatal or serious	1,075	277	964	142	2,458	6,259	314	606	5,080	138	236	12,633	603	15,813
All severities	7,110	2,023	4,173	684	13,990	38,826	1,804	3,819	21,141	568	1,063	67,221	6,596	88,961

1 Accident data by road class are not available for Northern Ireland.
2 Number of lanes in each direction.
3 Number of lanes in both directions.
4 Includes one way streets.
5 These are classified as junction accidents.
6 Includes unknown carriageway type and single track roads.
7 From 1st April 1991 responsibilty for Cumbria transferred from the North West Regional Office to the Northern Regional Office.
   The change to the road accident database was deferred until 1992. Consequently data prior to 1992 for both Northern and North West regions shown in this table in previous editions of RASER are not comparable with the 1994 data presented above.

14 Accidents: by road class, severity, region and county: 1981-85 average, 1993, 1994

Number

	Motorways			Trunk A roads			Principal A roads			All roads		
	Fatal	Fatal or serious	All severities	Fatal	Fatal or serious	All severities	Fatal	Fatal or serious	All severities	Fatal	Fatal or serious	All severities
Northern Region[1]												
1981-85	7	37	118	34	259	833	104	1,009	3,602	260	2,930	10,613
1993	9	36	186	43	193	987	74	624	3,270	211	1,876	9,936
1994	5	31	168	25	197	906	68	637	3,375	170	1,913	10,124
Cleveland[2]												
1981-85	0	0	0	4	19	97	18	174	770	42	423	2,137
1993	0	0	0	5	19	128	9	102	673	27	322	1,931
1994	0	0	0	4	13	121	11	84	687	32	242	2,015
Cumbria[1]												
1981-85	5	22	62	13	127	355	16	195	605	55	675	2,043
1993	2	18	70	23	101	378	14	118	550	53	386	1,818
1994	3	18	65	12	91	330	18	155	630	43	431	1,825
Durham												
1981-85	2	10	35	7	40	110	24	195	585	55	577	1,801
1993	6	12	74	4	12	135	11	86	520	36	273	1,882
1994	2	8	66	4	22	133	13	87	487	34	312	1,812
Northumberland[2]												
1981-85	0	0	0	7	45	163	11	87	280	35	313	1,043
1993	0	0	0	9	42	173	11	72	357	32	226	1,024
1994	0	0	0	1	46	133	8	69	334	18	236	954
Tyne and Wear												
1981-85	0	5	21	2	29	107	36	357	1,361	73	942	3,588
1993	1	6	42	2	19	173	29	246	1,170	63	669	3,281
1994	0	5	37	4	25	189	18	242	1,237	43	692	3,518
Yorkshire and Humberside Region												
1981-85	14	78	306	65	541	1,498	196	2,053	6,932	463	5,714	20,018
1993	17	77	518	43	324	1,290	156	1,381	6,828	351	3,810	19,276
1994	10	56	559	33	339	1,378	136	1,258	7,055	294	3,627	20,121
Humberside												
1981-85	2	10	33	8	72	243	28	308	1,201	73	996	3,894
1993	1	12	55	8	42	192	21	247	1,026	61	817	3,582
1994	2	10	57	3	53	201	23	199	972	53	748	3,718
North Yorkshire												
1981-85	0	3	8	24	239	467	29	474	1,048	82	1,423	3,128
1993	1	1	4	21	175	481	30	349	1,076	82	988	3,048
1994	0	1	5	16	180	521	33	310	1,100	73	912	3,156
South Yorkshire												
1981-85	4	26	110	10	75	250	42	420	1,654	103	1,123	4,631
1993	5	20	190	6	27	159	40	244	1,645	79	604	4,558
1994	4	22	177	4	22	143	28	264	1,786	57	617	4,629
West Yorkshire												
1981-85	7	39	155	23	155	538	96	851	3,030	205	2,172	8,365
1993	10	44	269	8	80	458	65	541	3,081	129	1,401	8,058
1994	4	23	320	10	84	513	52	485	3,197	111	1,350	8,618
East Midlands Region												
1981-85	15	129	390	97	792	2,350	158	1,770	5,721	443	5,334	17,379
1993	11	87	450	76	463	1,937	119	1,125	5,395	319	3,289	15,850
1994	4	72	428	65	461	2,026	113	1,114	5,369	308	3,231	16,091
Derbyshire												
1981-85	2	18	69	20	159	545	34	339	1,130	97	1,057	3,743
1993	2	14	112	21	100	507	26	146	1,077	69	477	3,504
1994	1	14	119	12	87	521	21	149	1,107	53	481	3,619
Leicestershire												
1981-85	6	24	93	16	115	360	32	330	1,198	93	1,042	3,702
1993	4	24	143	13	55	294	28	181	1,199	76	545	3,452
1994	1	13	146	10	43	288	23	194	1,190	71	515	3,546

1 From 1st April 1991 responsibilty for Cumbria transferred from the North West Regional Office to the Northern Regional Office.
   The change to the road accident database was deferred until 1992. However, for this table, data prior to 1992 have been changed to take account of the new boundaries.
2 This county contains no motorways.

31

14 Accidents: by road class, severity, region and county: 1981-85 average, 1993, 1994 (cont.)

Number

	Motorways			Trunk A roads			Principal A roads			All roads		
	Fatal	Fatal or serious	All severities	Fatal	Fatal or serious	All severities	Fatal	Fatal or serious	All severities	Fatal	Fatal or serious	All severities
Lincolnshire[1]												
1981-85	0	0	0	20	160	454	29	294	932	76	852	2,683
1993	0	0	0	14	84	279	27	255	923	65	641	2,439
1994	0	0	0	9	89	316	34	215	852	73	597	2,441
Northamptonshire												
1981-85	6	75	190	18	182	434	22	381	1,011	69	1,025	2,673
1993	4	38	138	8	77	290	15	226	848	41	599	2,211
1994	2	38	117	11	99	317	9	222	812	34	614	2,196
Nottinghamshire												
1981-85	1	11	38	22	175	557	41	426	1,450	108	1,359	4,577
1993	1	11	57	20	147	567	23	317	1,348	68	1,027	4,244
1994	0	7	46	23	143	584	26	334	1,408	77	1,024	4,289
Eastern Region												
1981-85	20	153	560	104	876	2,591	199	2,488	8,215	543	7,727	25,186
1993	24	177	1,059	66	555	2,319	158	1,503	7,843	427	4,697	24,016
1994	22	140	1,020	68	549	2,398	142	1,476	7,861	379	4,715	24,260
Bedfordshire												
1981-85	4	29	109	10	94	345	17	160	622	50	600	2,444
1993	1	13	92	12	58	281	13	92	582	44	341	2,036
1994	2	10	93	6	57	278	13	104	531	37	362	2,018
Buckinghamshire												
1981-85	5	38	120	3	36	110	27	318	1,001	63	843	2,617
1993	3	30	235	3	16	111	24	116	861	51	345	2,624
1994	3	21	214	5	25	136	21	114	890	38	330	2,725
Cambridgeshire												
1981-85	1	5	19	23	158	462	25	303	1,009	75	908	2,979
1993	1	7	22	14	117	444	24	242	1,089	60	716	3,279
1994	0	2	16	18	115	487	23	224	1,092	66	699	3,221
Essex												
1981-85	3	29	109	11	97	321	53	675	2,398	125	2,032	6,976
1993	7	49	237	14	95	469	38	356	2,090	88	1,147	6,364
1994	6	49	304	9	97	478	26	355	2,241	85	1,287	6,934
Hertfordshire												
1981-85	7	53	203	16	121	404	30	393	1,469	84	1,177	4,316
1993	12	78	473	8	74	308	19	279	1,352	56	880	4,219
1994	11	58	393	6	73	395	19	249	1,330	51	779	4,249
Norfolk[1]												
1981-85	0	0	0	21	190	461	27	360	910	82	1,207	3,110
1993	0	0	0	21	116	391	29	265	1,150	84	792	3,301
1994	0	0	0	14	137	400	25	272	982	59	828	3,018
Suffolk[1]												
1981-85	0	0	0	20	179	488	19	280	805	64	960	2,744
1993	0	0	0	16	79	315	11	153	719	44	476	2,193
1994	0	0	0	10	45	224	15	158	795	43	430	2,095
South East Region												
1981-85	29	205	652	109	800	2,453	282	3,500	12,091	677	9,327	32,192
1993	20	234	1,373	59	360	1,863	183	1,923	10,811	427	5,010	28,371
1994	17	191	1,430	56	395	2,034	190	1,976	11,286	406	5,087	29,824
Berkshire												
1981-85	10	69	215	7	61	195	24	321	1,167	71	942	3,263
1993	2	31	224	1	11	113	15	141	1,057	30	336	2,770
1994	5	26	230	0	12	123	25	144	1,073	47	337	2,924
East Sussex[1]												
1981-85	0	0	0	10	78	232	31	347	1,163	66	838	2,997
1993	0	0	0	7	53	200	19	204	1,077	51	514	2,701
1994	0	0	0	12	59	258	13	222	1,230	38	549	3,054

1 This county contains no motorways.

14 Accidents: by road class, severity, region and county: 1981-85 average, 1993, 1994 (cont.)

Number

	Motorways			Trunk A roads			Principal A roads			All roads		
	Fatal	Fatal or serious	All severities	Fatal	Fatal or serious	All severities	Fatal	Fatal or serious	All severities	Fatal	Fatal or serious	All severities
Hampshire												
1981-85	4	36	109	21	160	437	50	792	2,416	140	2,320	7,227
1993	2	60	276	12	64	261	40	425	2,283	103	1,248	6,692
1994	6	52	285	8	62	309	34	425	2,273	74	1,205	6,761
Isle of Wight[1]												
1981-85	0	0	0	0	0	0	4	70	214	8	155	495
1993	0	0	0	0	0	0	2	35	160	6	89	392
1994	0	0	0	0	0	0	3	44	203	5	94	471
Kent												
1981-85	7	49	162	21	175	539	63	779	2,543	142	2,053	6,819
1993	4	42	273	15	98	517	33	488	2,296	84	1,198	5,910
1994	1	35	219	9	114	566	39	444	2,378	80	1,230	6,161
Oxfordshire												
1981-85	1	6	12	24	164	521	26	279	801	71	871	2,531
1993	6	22	118	8	43	285	22	131	816	47	343	2,222
1994	3	18	129	9	44	262	24	139	815	46	336	2,202
Surrey												
1981-85	7	43	144	10	62	224	52	613	2,618	109	1,391	5,870
1993	5	77	467	4	39	241	31	334	2,134	56	828	5,136
1994	2	59	546	8	41	242	33	352	2,254	67	819	5,497
West Sussex												
1981-85	0	2	9	16	102	306	31	299	1,170	70	757	2,990
1993	1	2	15	12	52	246	21	165	988	50	454	2,548
1994	0	1	21	10	63	274	19	206	1,060	49	517	2,754
London												
1981-85	6	35	266	56	413	2,489	301	4,269	25,584	521	7,588	45,274
1993	3	61	435	45	643	4,230	141	2,959	19,565	277	5,842	38,533
1994	4	75	527	42	637	4,406	137	2,857	19,368	264	5,659	38,527
Inner London												
1981-85[2]	..	..	..	..	..	..	..	..	..	212	3,383	20,946
1993	0	3	39	13	249	1,676	67	1,522	10,306	116	2,659	18,000
1994	0	12	75	22	272	1,701	70	1,568	10,198	117	2,756	17,693
Outer London												
1981-85[2]	..	..	..	..	..	..	..	..	..	309	4,204	24,327
1993	3	58	396	32	394	2,554	74	1,437	9,259	161	3,183	20,533
1994	4	63	452	20	365	2,705	67	1,289	9,170	147	2,903	20,834
South West Region												
1981-85	17	127	344	62	585	1,586	197	2,475	7,390	440	6,697	19,847
1993	10	68	409	41	263	1,286	119	1,181	6,003	273	3,290	17,014
1994	14	79	427	52	251	1,249	128	1,090	6,169	294	3,017	17,150
Avon												
1981-85	8	50	124	3	29	61	41	450	1,415	86	1,149	3,596
1993	6	25	183	2	13	51	19	170	945	48	485	2,857
1994	5	23	183	3	8	42	15	122	926	39	401	2,711
Cornwall[1]												
1981-85	0	0	0	10	92	249	14	236	667	39	696	1,984
1993	0	0	0	4	37	225	16	136	678	31	357	1,966
1994	0	0	0	6	47	225	13	141	725	27	386	2,002
Devon												
1981-85	2	10	27	13	131	345	35	570	1,563	82	1,568	4,354
1993	0	12	46	10	66	292	16	227	1,156	44	804	3,957
1994	0	10	43	11	55	289	12	218	1,166	40	682	3,933
Dorset[1]												
1981-85	0	0	0	4	45	148	23	311	1,112	48	803	2,779
1993	0	0	0	6	32	147	21	158	999	47	422	2,450
1994	0	0	0	3	26	153	19	159	1,024	42	394	2,497

1 This county contains no motorways.
2 Trunk road data are not available for these years.

14 Accidents: by road class, severity, region and county: 1981-85 average, 1993, 1994 (cont.)

Number

	Motorways			Trunk A roads			Principal A roads			All roads		
	Fatal	Fatal or serious	All severities	Fatal	Fatal or serious	All severities	Fatal	Fatal or serious	All severities	Fatal	Fatal or serious	All severities
Gloucestershire												
1981-85	1	21	54	13	145	369	24	282	705	59	967	2,479
1993	0	5	54	8	39	255	15	131	679	35	376	2,039
1994	3	9	53	15	49	244	20	124	725	50	341	1,990
Somerset												
1981-85	3	17	43	6	48	117	29	295	789	57	666	1,783
1993	1	9	47	3	16	70	18	156	681	30	335	1,530
1994	3	13	60	4	15	57	20	139	711	39	339	1,697
Wiltshire												
1981-85	4	28	96	12	94	297	32	331	1,138	68	847	2,871
1993	3	17	79	8	60	246	14	203	865	38	511	2,215
1994	3	24	88	10	51	239	29	187	892	57	474	2,320
West Midlands Region												
1981-85	19	138	476	81	639	1,827	190	2,263	7,415	484	6,527	21,030
1993	21	160	788	47	330	1,515	129	1,316	7,194	307	3,769	19,783
1994	15	168	789	63	391	1,623	160	1,584	7,543	348	4,420	20,571
Hereford and Worcester												
1981-85	4	29	104	10	83	245	31	329	1,060	71	859	2,762
1993	3	17	101	10	55	249	26	181	918	55	432	2,446
1994	2	32	103	8	87	295	30	268	932	58	730	2,599
Shropshire												
1981-85	0	2	4	14	147	363	17	170	473	51	653	1,611
1993	1	7	16	16	73	213	10	102	441	41	370	1,521
1994	0	3	10	14	76	216	13	145	451	38	471	1,514
Staffordshire												
1981-85	8	36	146	25	163	602	36	405	1,577	105	1,209	4,813
1993	4	19	260	9	82	558	32	199	1,680	63	569	4,686
1994	8	39	232	22	98	622	46	238	1,803	92	668	4,928
Warwickshire												
1981-85	4	29	68	19	148	336	23	220	553	77	850	2,078
1993	3	67	197	7	76	249	9	137	616	28	585	2,250
1994	2	49	206	14	77	256	13	149	600	48	621	2,321
West Midlands												
1981-85	4	41	154	12	98	280	84	1,140	3,752	180	2,956	9,767
1993	10	50	214	5	44	246	52	697	3,539	120	1,813	8,880
1994	3	45	238	5	53	234	58	784	3,757	112	1,930	9,209
North West Region[1]												
1981-85	29	158	749	48	314	1,252	232	2,208	10,622	503	5,504	26,599
1993	25	147	1,209	22	228	1,409	180	1,666	11,909	352	4,168	29,363
1994	27	181	1,368	35	280	1,519	149	1,731	12,166	350	4,525	30,120
Cheshire												
1981-85	8	44	198	17	92	400	32	277	1,436	83	778	3,913
1993	8	32	353	6	69	402	41	204	1,537	75	520	4,137
1994	7	49	388	12	102	426	27	319	1,619	68	865	4,364
Greater Manchester												
1981-85	10	59	337	6	50	214	90	971	4,966	178	2,149	11,127
1993	9	48	491	3	23	219	66	663	5,424	132	1,497	12,196
1994	11	53	564	5	28	253	45	581	5,522	107	1,338	12,373
Lancashire												
1981-85	8	40	147	17	113	377	60	554	2,161	135	1,478	5,803
1993	6	53	222	7	90	396	41	460	2,168	81	1,281	5,822
1994	7	63	258	12	107	443	39	517	2,348	101	1,482	6,409
Merseyside												
1981-85	3	14	67	7	59	260	50	406	2,059	107	1,099	5,756
1993	2	14	143	6	46	392	32	339	2,780	64	870	7,208
1994	2	16	158	6	43	397	38	314	2,677	74	840	6,974

1 From 1st April 1991 responsibilty for Cumbria transferred from the North West Regional Office to the Northern Regional Office.
The change to the road accident database was deferred until 1992. However, for this table, data prior to 1992 have been changed to take account of the new boundaries.

14 Accidents: by road class, severity, region and county: 1981-85 average, 1993, 1994 (cont.)

Number

	Motorways			Trunk A roads			Principal A roads			All roads		
	Fatal	Fatal or serious	All severities	Fatal	Fatal or serious	All severities	Fatal	Fatal or serious	All severities	Fatal	Fatal or serious	All severities
England												
1981-85	156	1,059	3,860	654	5,220	16,880	1,859	22,035	87,572	4,333	57,347	218,137
1993	140	1,047	6,427	464	3,359	16,836	1,259	13,678	78,818	2,944	35,751	202,142
1994	118	993	6,716	439	3,500	17,539	1,223	13,723	80,192	2,813	36,194	206,788
Wales												
1981-85	5	38	124	62	620	1,746	86	984	3,427	233	3,082	10,583
1993	2	17	153	43	333	1,390	61	571	3,121	167	1,747	10,049
1994	6	26	179	48	329	1,487	73	570	3,201	194	1,776	10,536
Scotland												
1981-85	16	110	265	138	1,010	2,433	228	2,751	7,438	581	7,412	20,471
1993	17	74	283	93	614	2,005	131	1,344	5,657	359	4,003	16,674
1994	11	99	330	86	631	1,894	121	1,520	5,568	319	4,642	16,777
Great Britain												
1981-85	177	1,207	4,249	854	6,850	21,058	2,173	25,769	98,436	5,147	67,842	249,192
1993	159	1,138	6,863	600	4,306	20,231	1,451	15,593	87,596	3,470	41,501	228,865
1994	135	1,118	7,225	573	4,460	20,920	1,417	15,813	88,961	3,326	42,612	234,101

15 Accidents and casualties by severity: vehicles involved by vehicle type: road length: all by selected individual motorways[1]: 1994

| | Accidents | | | Casualties | | | Vehicles involved | | | | Kilo-metres open at December 1994[3] |
	Fatal	Serious	All severities	Fatal	Serious	All severities	Two-wheel motor vehicles	Cars and LGV	HGV	All vehicles[2]	
England											
M1, M10	16	114	942	20	171	1,553	42	1,836	316	2,226	322
M45	0	3	5	0	3	8	0	6	0	6	17
M2	0	11	61	0	20	99	7	101	21	129	43
M3	4	31	189	4	37	264	15	316	43	379	90
M4	13	76	584	14	109	894	41	1,080	128	1,268	191
M5	10	69	348	11	104	643	17	640	86	758	263
M6	23	134	987	27	193	1,796	23	1,903	495	2,448	383
M11	5	29	151	5	45	231	7	243	43	296	85
M18	0	3	40	0	3	72	0	64	18	85	46
M20	1	15	92	1	19	152	6	118	27	153	84
M23	0	13	128	0	14	277	3	309	11	326	28
M25	6	101	926	8	128	1,402	51	1,865	312	2,250	186
M26	0	4	8	0	7	17	3	6	2	11	16
M27, M271, M275	3	21	159	3	25	237	10	348	23	386	60
M40	6	34	284	6	50	483	15	503	60	589	147
M42	2	26	121	3	41	204	2	266	36	307	72
M50	0	2	13	0	2	16	0	10	11	22	35
M53	1	6	69	1	6	102	8	116	10	135	32
M54	0	8	20	0	10	31	2	28	2	32	36
M55	1	7	29	1	10	53	1	53	1	55	19
M56	2	18	120	2	24	191	7	232	31	273	60
M57	1	5	34	1	7	58	0	51	12	66	17
M58	0	2	17	0	2	26	0	27	4	31	19
M61	4	14	88	5	26	175	1	165	28	196	40
M62	10	45	500	11	62	821	10	943	216	1,175	175
M63	2	7	120	3	10	159	3	227	31	263	26
M65	0	4	35	0	8	58	1	61	3	65	22
M66	1	2	34	1	2	51	0	58	12	72	19
M69	0	2	21	0	2	30	2	30	6	38	28
M180 & M181	0	5	34	0	6	47	0	51	17	69	45
Other motorways	2	15	137	2	15	196	8	245	29	287	35
Motorways	113	826	6,296	129	1,161	10,346	285	11,901	2,034	14,396	2,638
A(M) roads	5	49	420	6	57	621	43	732	75	860	201
Total (inc A(M) roads)	118	875	6,716	135	1,218	10,967	328	12,633	2,109	15,256	2,839
Wales											
Motorways	6	20	177	6	27	269	6	318	53	381	119
A(M) roads	0	0	2	0	0	2	2	1	0	3	3
Total (inc A(M) roads)	6	20	179	6	27	271	8	319	53	384	123
Scotland											
Motorways	11	87	328	16	112	510	10	544	76	634	
A(M) roads	0	1	2	0	1	2	0	2	2	4	
Total (inc A(M) roads)	11	88	330	16	113	512	10	546	78	638	305[4]
Great Britain											
Motorways	130	933	6,801	151	1,300	11,125	301	12,763	2,163	15,411	2,757
A(M) roads	5	50	424	6	58	625	45	735	77	867	204
Total (inc A(M) roads)	135	983	7,225	157	1,358	11,750	346	13,498	2,240	16,278	2,962

1 Casualty and accident data by road class are not available for Northern Ireland.
2 Includes pedal cycles, buses and coaches and other vehicles.
3 Excluding slip roads. Data for England from 1994 onwards supplied by DOT Statistics Directorate. Data for Wales from Welsh Office and Scotland from Scottish Office.
4 As at 1 April 1994.

16 Distribution of accidents by road class and region [1] : 1993, 1994

percentage (row sums = 100)

	Motorways		Trunk roads		Principal roads		Other roads	
	1993	1994	1993	1994	1993	1994	1993	1994
Northern [2]	1.9	1.7	9.9	8.9	32.9	33.3	55.3	56.1
Yorkshire and Humberside	2.7	2.8	6.7	6.8	35.4	35.1	55.2	55.3
East Midlands	2.8	2.7	12.2	12.6	34.0	33.4	50.9	51.4
Eastern	4.4	4.2	9.7	9.9	32.7	32.4	53.3	53.5
South Eastern	4.8	4.8	6.6	6.8	38.1	37.8	50.5	50.5
Greater London	1.1	1.4	11.0	11.4	50.8	50.3	37.1	36.9
South West	2.4	2.5	7.6	7.3	35.3	36.0	54.2	54.3
West Midlands	4.0	3.8	7.7	7.9	36.4	36.7	52.0	51.6
North West [2]	4.1	4.5	4.8	5.0	40.6	40.4	50.5	50.0
England	3.2	3.2	8.3	8.5	39.0	38.8	49.5	49.5
Wales	1.5	1.7	13.8	14.1	31.1	30.4	53.6	53.8
Scotland	1.7	2.0	12.0	11.3	33.9	33.2	52.4	53.6
Great Britain	3.0	3.1	8.8	8.9	38.3	38.0	49.9	50.0

1 Accident data by road class are not available for Northern Ireland.
2 From 1st April 1991 responsibilty for Cumbria transferred from the North West Regional Office to the Northern Regional Office.
 The change to the road accident database was deferred until 1992. Consequently, the data prior to 1992 for both the Northern and North West regions
 shown in this table in previous editions of RASER are not comparable with the 1994 data presented above.

17 Motor vehicles, population, area and road length (motorways and built-up and non built-up roads: by trunk and principal): by region: 1994

Thousands/ number

	Motor vehicles currently licensed [1] (thousands)	Population [2] mid year (home) (thousands)	Area in hectares (thousands)	Road length (kilometres)				
				Motorways [3][4]	Built-up [4]		Non built-up [4]	
					Trunk	Principal	Trunk	Principal
Northern [5]	1,115	3,102	1,540	152	55	600	749	1,445
Yorkshire and Humberside	2,002	5,014	1,542	290	105	1,170	665	1,429
East Midlands	1,760	4,082	1,563	185	147	777	1,086	1,959
Eastern	2,995	5,844	2,100	316	103	1,103	1,209	2,198
South East	3,492	7,085	1,722	567	70	1,611	772	2,469
Greater London	2,716	6,933	158	60	211	1,353	141	45
South West	2,409	4,768	2,385	302	53	1,208	987	2,802
West Midlands	2,551	5,290	1,301	380	102	1,140	750	1,612
North West [5]	2,598	6,412	733	486	94	1,664	413	988
England	21,638	48,532	13,044	2,744	940	10,626	6,771	14,947
Wales	1,177	2,906	2,077	123	202	866	1,375	1,796
Scotland	1,900	5,120	7,717	305	214	1,244	2,646	6,311
Great Britain	24,715	56,558	22,838	3,172	1,356	12,736	10,792	23,054
Northern Ireland	596	1,632	1,416	118	499[6]		1725[6]	
United Kingdom	25,311	58,190	24,254	3,290	1,356	12,736	10,792	23,054

1 Includes all vehicles licensed to use public roads. From 1992, estimates of licensed stock are taken from the Department of Transport's Statistics Directorate
 Information Database.
2 Final 1993 population estimates.
3 Excluding slip roads. Total for England includes figures for non-trunk motorways not included in regional totals.
 Data for Wales from Welsh Office and Scotland from Scottish Office.
4 As at April 1994. Road length figures taken from DOT Transport Statistics Report "Road Lengths in Great Britain 1994".
5 From 1st April 1991 responsibilty for Cumbria transferred from the North West Regional Office to the Northern Regional Office.
 Consequently, the data prior to 1992 for both the Northern and North West regions shown in this table in previous editions of RASER are not comparable
 with the 1994 data presented above.
6 Trunk and Principal road length data are not available for Northern Ireland, data are for all A roads.

37

18 Motor traffic distribution between regions [1] : by motorway and built-up and non built-up trunk and principal roads: 1992-1994 average

percentage [2]

| | Motorways | Built-up 'A' | | Non built-up 'A' | | All major roads |
		Trunk	Principal	Trunk	Principal	
Northern [3]	1	1	3	5	5	3
Yorkshire & Humberside	8	7	9	8	7	8
East Midlands	6	10	5	11	9	8
Eastern	10	6	7	17	13	11
South East	25	6	14	14	21	18
Greater London	3	33	16	4	0	7
South West	8	3	8	9	13	9
West Midlands	13	8	10	7	8	9
North West [3]	17	8	15	7	8	12
England	92	83	88	81	84	86
Wales	3	8	4	7	5	5
Scotland	5	9	8	12	10	9
Great Britain	100	100	100	100	100	100

1 Traffic data by road class are not available for Northern Ireland.
2 Figures have been rounded to the nearest whole number.
3 From 1st April 1991 responsibilty for Cumbria transferred from the North West Regional Office to the Northern Regional Office.
   The change to the road accident database was deferred until 1992.

19 Motor traffic distribution between motorways, built-up and non built-up trunk and principal roads: by region [1] : 1992-1994 average

percentage [2]

| | Motorways | Built-up 'A' | | Non built-up 'A' | | All major roads |
		Trunk	Principal	Trunk	Principal	
Northern [3]	9	1	26	31	33	100
Yorkshire & Humberside	24	3	31	22	20	100
East Midlands	20	5	19	31	26	100
Eastern	22	2	17	33	26	100
South East	34	1	21	18	26	100
Greater London	9	17	58	14	2	100
South West	22	1	23	22	32	100
West Midlands	34	3	28	16	19	100
North West [3]	36	3	34	13	15	100
England	26	4	27	21	22	100
Wales	14	6	23	33	24	100
Scotland	15	4	24	31	26	100
Great Britain	24	4	27	23	23	100

1 Traffic data by road class are not available for Northern Ireland.
2 Figures have been rounded to the nearest whole number.
3 From 1st April 1991 responsibilty for Cumbria transferred from the North West Regional Office to the Northern Regional Office.
   The change to the road accident database was deferred until 1992.

Definitions

Accident: One involving personal injury occurring on the public highway (including footways) in which a road vehicle is involved and which becomes known to the police within 30 days of its occurrence. The vehicle need not be moving and it need not be in collision with anything. One accident may give rise to several *casualties*. Damage-only accidents are not included in this publication.

'A' Roads: All purpose *trunk* roads and *principal* local authority roads.

Adults: Persons aged 16 years and over.

Built-up Roads: Roads with speed limits (ignoring temporary limits) of 40 mph or less. 'Non built-up roads' refer to those with speed limits of over 40 mph. *Motorways* are included with non built-up roads unless otherwise stated. In tables where data for *motorways* are shown separately, the totals for built-up and non built-up roads exclude *motorway accidents*. In comparing such tables with those involving a built-up/non built-up split only, negligible error will be made by assuming that *motorway accidents* were all on non built-up roads.

Cars: Includes taxis, estate cars, invalid tricycles, three and four-wheeled cars, minibuses and motor caravans.

Casualty: A person *killed* or injured in an *accident*. Casualties are classified as either *killed, seriously injured* or *slightly injured*.

Children: Persons under 16 years of age.

Fatal Accident: One in which at least one person is *killed* (but excluding confirmed suicides).

Heavy goods vehicles (HGV): Prior to 1994 these were defined as those vehicles over 1.524 tonnes unladen weight and included vehicles with six or more tyres, some four-wheel vehicles with extra large bodies and larger rear tyres and tractor units travelling without their usual trailer. From 1 January 1994 the weight definition changed to those vehicles over 3.5 tonnes maximum permissible gross vehicle weight (gvw).

Light goods vehicles (LGV): Prior to 1994 these were defined as those vehicles not over 1.524 tonnes unladen weight. From 1 January 1994 the weight definition changed to those vehicles not over 3.5 tonnes maximum permissible gross vehicle weight. Light vans mainly include vehicles of the van type constructed on a car chassis.

Killed: Human *casualties* who sustained injuries resulting in death within 30 days of the *accident*.

KSI: *Killed* or *seriously injured*.

Licensed Vehicles: The stock of vehicles currently licensed on 31 December, when the annual census is taken at the Driver and Vehicle Licensing Agency (DVLA).

London: Where possible, data for London have been split into Inner and Outer London. Inner London comprises the City of London and the boroughs of Westminster, Camden, Islington, Hackney, Tower Hamlets, Lewisham, Southwark, Lambeth, Wandsworth, Hammersmith, Kensington and Chelsea, Newham and Haringey. Outer London is all other London boroughs, and includes Heathrow Airport. This definition conforms to that used by the Office of Population Censuses and Surveys (OPCS).

Major Roads: These are *motorways*, A(M) and *A class roads* (both *trunk* and *principal*).

Motorcyclist: Riders and passengers of two-wheeled motor vehicles.

Motorways: Motorways and A(M) roads except where otherwise noted. The motorway lengths given in Tables 15 and 17 are main line lengths and exclude associated slip roads.

Motorway Accident: *Accidents* on *motorways* include those on associated slip roads and those at junctions between *motorways* and other roads where the *accident* cannot be clearly allocated to the other road.

Other Roads: These are 'B' and 'C' class roads and unclassified roads, including 'road class not reported'.

Pedal cycle: Includes tandems, tricycles and toy cycles ridden on the carriageway. Also includes battery-assisted cycles and tricycles with a maximum speed of 15 mph.

Pedal cyclist: Riders of *pedal cycles* including any passengers.

Pedestrians: Also includes persons riding toy cycles on the footway, persons pushing bicycles or pushing or pulling other vehicles or operating pedestrian-controlled vehicles, those leading or herding animals, occupants of prams or wheelchairs, and persons who alight safely from vehicles and are subsequently injured.

Population: The population data used in calculating rates are the final mid-1993 estimates. Mid-year estimates for 1994 were not available at the time of going to publication. The estimates include residents who are temporarily outside the country, and exclude both foreign visitors and members of HM armed forces who are stationed abroad.

Principal Roads: Roads for which County Councils (Regional and Island Authorities in Scotland) are the Highway Authority. The classified *principal roads* (which include local authority *motorways*) are those of regional and urban strategic importance.

Serious Accident: One in which at least one person is *seriously injured* but no person (other than a confirmed suicide) is killed.

Serious Injury: An injury for which a person is detained in hospital as an 'in-patient', or any of the following injuries whether or not the *casualty* was detained in hospital: fractures, concussion, internal injuries, crushings, severe cuts and lacerations, severe general shock requiring medical treatment, injuries causing death 30 or more days after the *accident*. An injured *casualty* is coded as seriously or *slightly injured* by the police on the basis of information available within a short time of the *accident*. This generally will not include the result of a medical examination, but may include the fact of being detained in hospital, the reasons for which may vary from area to area.

Severity: Of an *accident,* the severity of the most severely injured *casualty* (either fatal, serious or slight); of a casualty, killed, seriously injured or slightly injured.

Slight Accident: One in which at least one person is *slightly injured*, but no person is *killed* or *seriously injured.*

Slight Injury: An injury of a minor character such as a sprain, bruise or cut which are not judged to be severe, or slight shock requiring roadside attention only.

Two-wheel motor vehicles: Mopeds, motor scooters and motor cycles (including motor cycle combinations.

Trunk Roads: Roads comprising the national network of through routes for which the Secretary of State for Transport in England and the Secretaries of State for Scotland and Wales are the highway authorities. The network contains both *motorways*, which legally are special roads reserved for certain classes of traffic, and all-purpose roads which are open to all classes of traffic.

Department of Transport

Accident Record Attendant Circumstances

1.1 Record Type `1`

11 New accident record
15 Amended accident record

1.2 Police Force

1.3 Accident Ref No

1.5 Number of Vehicle Records

1.6 Number of Casualty Records

1.7 Date

Day Month Year

1.9 Time of Day

Hours Mins
24 hour

1.10 Local Authority

1.11 Location

10 digit OS Grid Reference number

Easting Northing

1.12 1st Road Class

1 Motorway
2 A (M)
3 A
4 B
5 C
6 Unclassified

1.13 1st Road Number

1.14 Carriageway Type or Markings

1 Roundabout - on circular highway
2 One way street
3 Dual carriageway - 2 lanes
4 Dual carriageway - 3 or more lanes
5 Single carriageway - single track road
6 Single carriageway - 2 lanes (one in each direction)
7 Single carriageway - 3 lanes (two way capacity)
8 Single carriageway - 4 or more lanes (two way capacity)
9 Unknown

1.15 Speed Limit `0` mph

1.16 Junction Detail `0`

00 Not at or within 20 metres of junction
01 Roundabout
02 Mini roundabout
03 T or staggered junction
04 Y junction
05 Slip road
06 Crossroads
07 Multiple junction
08 Using private drive or entrance
09 Other junction

Junction Accidents Only

1.17 Junction Control

1 Authorised person
2 Automatic traffic signal
3 Stop sign
4 Give way sign or markings
5 Uncontrolled

1.18 2nd Road Class

1 Motorway
2 A (M)
3 A
4 B
5 C
6 Unclassified

1.19 2nd Road Number

1.20 Pedestrian Crossing Facilities `0`

00 No crossing facility within 50 metres
01 Zebra crossing
02 Zebra crossing controlled by school crossing patrol
03 Zebra crossing controlled by other authorised person
04 Pelican or puffin crossing
05 Other light controlled crossing
06 Other site controlled by school crossing patrol
07 Other site controlled by other authorised person
08 Central refuge - no other controls
09 Footbridge or subway

1.21 Light Conditions

1 Daylight: street lights present
2 Daylight: no street lighting
3 Daylight: street lighting unknown
4 Darkness: street lights present and lit
5 Darkness: street lights present but unlit
6 Darkness: no street lighting
7 Darkness: street lighting unknown

1.22 Weather

1 Fine without high winds
2 Raining without high winds
3 Snowing without high winds
4 Fine with high winds
5 Raining with high winds
6 Snowing with high winds
7 Fog or mist - if hazard
8 Other
9 Unknown

1.23 Road Surface Condition

1 Dry
2 Wet / Damp
3 Snow
4 Frost / Ice
5 Flood (surface water over 3cm deep)

1.24 Special Conditions at Site

0 None
1 Automatic traffic signal out
2 Automatic traffic signal partially defective
3 Permanent road signing defective or obscured
4 Road works present
5 Road surface defective

1.25 Carriageway Hazards

0 None
1 Dislodged vehicle load in carriageway
2 Other object in carriageway
3 Involvement with previous accident
4 Dog in carriageway
5 Other animal or pedestrian in carriageway

1.27 DOT Special Projects

Vehicle Record

2.1 Record Type
☐ 2

21 New vehicle record
25 Amended vehicle record

2.2 Police Force
☐☐

2.3 Accident Ref No
☐☐☐☐☐

2.4 Vehicle Ref No
☐☐

2.5 Type of Vehicle
☐☐

01 Pedal cycle
02 Moped
03 Motor scooter
04 Motor cycle
05 Combination
06 Invalid tricycle
07 Other three-
   wheeled car
08 Taxi
09 Car (four-wheeled)
10 Minibus / Motor caravan
11 Bus or coach
12 Light goods vehicle
13 Heavy goods vehicle
14 Other motor vehicle
15 Other non-motor vehicle

2.6 Towing and Articulation
☐

0 No tow or articulation
1 Articulated vehicle
2 Double or multiple trailer
3 Caravan
4 Single trailer
5 Other tow

2.7 Manoeuvres
☐☐

01 Reversing
02 Parked
03 Waiting to go ahead
   but held up
04 Stopping
05 Starting
06 U turn
07 Turning left
08 Waiting to turn left
09 Turning right
10 Waiting to turn right
11 Changing lane to left
12 Changing lane to
   right
13 Overtaking moving
   vehicle on its offside
14 Overtaking stationary
   vehicle on its offside
15 Overtaking on nearside
16 Going ahead left
   hand bend
17 Going ahead right
   hand bend
18 Going ahead other

2.8 Vehicle Movement Compass Point
From To ☐ ☐

Parked:
not at kerb ☐0 0
at kerb * ☐0
* code 1 - 8

1 N   5 S
2 NE 6 SW
3 E   7 W
4 SE 8 NW

2.9 Vehicle Location at Time of Accident
01 Leaving the main road
02 Entering the main road
03 On the main road
04 On the minor road
05 On service road
06 On lay-by or hard shoulder
07 Entering lay-by or hard shoulder
08 Leaving lay-by or hard shoulder
09 On cycleway
10 Not on carriageway

2.10 Junction Location of Vehicle at First Impact
0 Not at junction (or within 20 metres)
1 Vehicle approaching junction or parked at
   junction approach
2 Vehicle in middle of junction
3 Vehicle cleared junction or parked at junction
   exit
4 Did not impact

2.11 Skidding and Overturning
0 No skidding, jack-knifing or overturning
1 Skidded
2 Skidded and overturned
3 Jack-knifed
4 Jack-knifed and overturned
5 Overturned

2.12 Hit Object in Carriageway
☐☐

00 None
01 Previous accident
02 Road works
03 Parked vehicle - lit
04 Parked vehicle - unlit
05 Bridge - roof
06 Bridge - side
07 Bollard / Refuge
08 Open door of vehicle
09 Central island of roundabout
10 Kerb
11 Other object

2.13 Vehicle Leaving Carriageway
☐

0 Did not leave carriageway
1 Left carriageway nearside
2 Left carriageway nearside and rebounded
3 Left carriageway straight ahead at junction
4 Left carriageway offside onto central reservation
5 Left carriageway offside onto central reservation
   and rebounded
6 Left carriageway offside and crossed central
   reservation
7 Left carriageway offside
8 Left carriageway offside and rebounded

2.14 Hit Object Off Carriageway
☐

00 None
01 Road sign / Traffic signal
02 Lamp post
03 Telegraph pole / Electricity pole
04 Tree
05 Bus stop / Bus shelter
06 Central crash barrier
07 Nearside or offside crash barrier
08 Submerged in water (completely)
09 Entered ditch
10 Other permanent object

2.16 First Point of Impact
☐

0 Did not impact 3 Offside
1 Front   4 Nearside
2 Back

2.17 Other Vehicle Hit
☐☐
Ref no of other vehicle

2.18 Part(s) Damaged
☐
☐
☐

0 None   4 Nearside
1 Front   5 Roof
2 Back   6 Underside
3 Offside 7 All four sides

2.21 Sex of Driver
☐

1 Male   3 Not traced
2 Female

2.22 Age of Driver
☐☐ Years
Estimated if necessary

2.23 Breath Test
☐

0 Not applicable 3 Not requested
1 Positive   4 Failed to provide
2 Negative   5 Driver not contacted at time

2.24 Hit and Run
☐

0 Other   2 Non-stop, vehicle not hit
1 Hit and Run

2.25 DOT Special Projects
☐

2.26 Vehicle Registration Mark (VRM)
☐☐

VRM or one of the following codes
2 Foreign / Diplomatic 4 Trade plates
3 Military   9 Unknown

Casualty Record

3.1 Record Type

3

- 31 New casualty record
- 35 Amended casualty record

3.2 Police Force

3.3 Accident Ref No

3.4 Vehicle Ref No

3.5 Casualty Ref No

3.6 Casualty Class

- 1 Driver or rider
- 2 Vehicle or pillion passenger
- 3 Pedestrian

3.7 Sex of Casualty

- 1 Male
- 2 Female

3.8 Age of Casualty

Years

Estimated if necessary

3.9 Severity of Casualty

- 1 Fatal
- 2 Serious
- 3 Slight

3.10 Pedestrian Location

- 00 Not a pedestrian
- 01 In carriageway, crossing on pedestrian crossing
- 02 In carriageway, crossing within zig-zag lines at crossing approach
- 03 In carriageway, crossing within zig-zag lines at crossing exit
- 04 In carriageway, crossing elsewhere within 50 metres of pedestrian crossing
- 05 In carriageway, crossing elsewhere
- 06 On footway or verge
- 07 On refuge, central island or central reservation
- 08 In centre of carriageway, not on refuge, central island or central reservation
- 09 In carriageway, not crossing
- 10 Unknown or other

3.11 Pedestrian Movement

- 0 Not a pedestrian
- 1 Crossing from driver's nearside
- 2 Crossing from driver's nearside - masked by parked or stationary vehicle
- 3 Crossing from driver's offside
- 4 Crossing from driver's offside - masked by parked or stationary vehicle
- 5 In carriageway, stationary - not crossing (standing or playing)
- 6 In carriageway, stationary - not crossing (standing or playing), masked by parked or stationary vehicle
- 7 Walking along in carriageway - facing traffic
- 8 Walking along in carriageway - back to traffic
- 9 Unknown or other

3.12 Pedestrian Direction

Compass point bound

- 1 N
- 2 NE
- 3 E
- 4 SE
- 5 S
- 6 SW
- 7 W
- 8 NW
- 0 Standing still

3.13 School Pupil Casualty

- 1 School pupil on journey to or from school
- 0 Other

3.15 Car Passenger

- 0 Not a car passenger
- 1 Front seat car passenger
- 2 Rear seat car passenger

3.16 Bus or Coach Passenger

- 0 Not a bus or coach passenger
- 1 Boarding
- 2 Alighting
- 3 Standing passenger
- 4 Seated passenger

3.17 DOT Special Projects